UNDERGROUND CLINICAL VIGNETTES

PHARMACOLOGY

Classic Clinical Cases
for USMLE Step 1 & 2 Review [100 cases, 1st ed]

VIKAS BHUSHAN, MD
University of California, San Francisco, Class of 1991
Series Editor, Diagnostic Radiologist

CHIRAG AMIN, MD
University of Miami, Class of 1996
Orlando Regional Medical Center, Resident in Orthopaedic Surgery

TAO LE, MD
University of California, San Francisco, Class of 1996
Yale-New Haven Hospital, Resident in Internal Medicine

HOANG NGUYEN
Northwestern University, Medical Scientist Training Program

JOSE M. FIERRO, MD
La Salle University, Mexico City
Brookdale University Hospital, New York, Intern in Medicine/Pediatrics

KRIS ALDEN
University of Illinois - Chicago, Medical Scientist Training Program

VISHAL PALL, MBBS
Government Medical College, Chandigarh, India, Class of 1996

Cover Design: Ashley Pound

Editor: Andrea Fellows

This book was created with MS Word97 using the following typefaces: Garamond, Futura Medium, and Futura ExtraBold. The cases were developed in a master table and converted into pages by a macro written by Alex Grimm. The camera-ready copy was created on a Lexmark Optra R by Vikas Bhushan.

Printed in the USA

ISBN: 1-890061-12-3

Contributors

SAMIR MEHTA
Temple University, Class of 2000

ALEA EUSEBIO
UCLA School of Medicine, Class of 2000

VIPAL SONI
UCLA School of Medicine, Class of 1999

Acknowledgments

Throughout the production of this book, we have had the support of many friends and colleagues. Special thanks to our administrative assistant, Gianni Le Nguyen. For expert computer support, Tarun Mathur (hardware) and Alex Grimm (software). For editing, proofreading, and assistance, thanks to Cecilia Wieslander, Ken Lin and Dr. Bertram Katzung (UC San Francisco).

Table of Contents

Case	Subspecialty	Name
42	ID	Fluoroquinolone Side Effects
43	ID	Ketoconazole Side Effects
44	ID	Penicillin Allergic Reaction
45	ID	Rifampin Side Effects
46	ID	Zidovudine Toxicity
47	Neurology	Anticonvulsant Osteomalacia
48	Neurology	Barbiturate Intoxication
49	Neurology	Carbamazepine Side Effects
50	Neurology	Fetal Alcohol Syndrome
51	Neurology	Ketamine Side Effects
52	Neurology	Levodopa Side Effects
53	Neurology	MPTP-Induced Parkinson's Disease
54	Neurology	Phenytoin Overdose
55	Psychiatry	Amphetamine Withdrawal
56	Psychiatry	Lithium Side Effects
57	Psychiatry	Neuroleptic Malignant Syndrome
58	Psychiatry	Neuroleptic Side Effects
59	Psychiatry	Tardive Dyskinesia
60	Psychiatry	Tricyclic Antidepressant Overdose
61	Pulmonary	Acute Asthma
62	Pulmonary	Amiodarone Side Effects
63	Toxicology	Acetaminophen Overdose
64	Toxicology	Aluminum Toxicity
65	Toxicology	Ammonia Overdose
66	Toxicology	Amphetamine Abuse
67	Toxicology	Arsenic Poisoning
68	Toxicology	Caffeine Intoxication
69	Toxicology	Cannabis Intoxication
70	Toxicology	Carbon Monoxide Poisoning
71	Toxicology	Cocaine Abuse
72	Toxicology	Cocaine Withdrawal
73	Toxicology	Cyanide Poisoning
74	Toxicology	Cyclophosphamide Side Effects
75	Toxicology	Cyclosporine Side Effects
76	Toxicology	Digitalis Intoxication
77	Toxicology	Drug-Induced Systemic Lupus
78	Toxicology	Ethylene Glycol Ingestion
79	Toxicology	Gentamicin Side Effects
80	Toxicology	Heroin Overdose
81	Toxicology	Ipecac Toxicity
82	Toxicology	Iron Overdose
83	Toxicology	Laxative Abuse
84	Toxicology	Lead Poisoning
85	Toxicology	Malignant Hyperthermia
86	Toxicology	Mercury Poisoning
87	Toxicology	Methanol Poisoning

Case	Subspecialty	Name
88	Toxicology	Mushroom Poisoning
89	Toxicology	Nicotine Withdrawal
90	Toxicology	NSAID Toxicity
91	Toxicology	Opioid Withdrawal
92	Toxicology	Parathion Poisoning
93	Toxicology	PCP Toxicity
94	Toxicology	Propranolol Toxicity
95	Toxicology	Reye's Syndrome
96	Toxicology	Salicylate Toxicity
97	Toxicology	Thalidomide Exposure
98	Urology	Drug-Induced Tubulointerstitial Disease
99	Urology	Loop Diuretic Side Effect
100	Urology	Renal Papillary Necrosis

Preface

This series was developed to address the increasing number of clinical vignette questions on the USMLE Step 1 and Step 2. It is designed to supplement and complement *First Aid for the USMLE Step 1* (Appleton & Lange).

Each book uses a series of approximately 100 "**supra-prototypical**" **cases as a way to condense testable facts and associations.** The clinical vignettes in this series are designed to incorporate as many testable facts as possible into a cohesive and memorable clinical picture. The vignettes represent composites drawn from general and specialty textbooks, reference books, thousands of USMLE style questions and the personal experience of the authors and reviewers.

Although each case tends to present all the signs, symptoms, and diagnostic findings for a particular illness, **patients generally will not present with such a "complete" picture either clinically or on the Step 1 exam.** Cases are not meant to simulate a potential real patient or an exam vignette. All the **boldfaced "buzzwords" are for learning purposes** and are not necessarily expected to be found in any one patient with the disease.

Definitions of selected important terms are placed within the vignettes in (= SMALL CAPS) in parentheses. Other parenthetical remarks often refer to the pathophysiology or mechanism of disease. The format should also help students learn to present cases succinctly during oral "bullet" presentations on clinical rotations. The cases are meant to be read as a condensed review, not as a primary reference.

The information provided in this book has been prepared with a great deal of thought and careful research. This book should not, however, be considered as your sole source of information. Corrections, suggestions and submissions of new cases are encouraged and will be acknowledged and incorporated in future editions (see How to Contribute).

How to Contribute

We invite your corrections and suggestions for the next edition of this book. **For the first submission of each factual correction or new vignette, you will receive a personal acknowledgment and a free copy of the revised book.**

We prefer that you submit corrections or suggestions via electronic mail to **vbhushan@aol.com**. Please include "Underground Vignettes" as the subject of your message.

For corrections to this book, visit our Student to Student Medical Publishing Site at:

http://www.s2smed.com

If you do not have access to e-mail, use the following mailing address:
S2S Medical Publishing, 1015 Gayley Ave, Box 1113, Los Angeles, CA 90024 USA.

Abbreviations

ID/CC	identification and chief complaint
HPI	history of present illness
PE	physical exam

ABGs	arterial blood gases
CBC	complete blood count
ECG	electrocardiography
EMG	electromyography
LYTES	electrolytes
PBS	peripheral blood smear
PE	physical exam
PFTs	pulmonary function tests
UA	urinalysis
VS	vital signs

Angio	angiography
BE	barium enema
CT	computerized tomography
CXR	chest x-ray
Echo	echocardiography
EEG	electroencephalography
EGD	esophagogastroduodenoscopy
ERCP	endoscopic retrograde cholangiopancreatography
FNA	fine needle aspiration
HIDA	hepatoiminodiacetic acid [scan]
IVP	intravenous pyelography
KUB	kidneys/ureter/bladder
LP	lumbar puncture
Mammo	mammography
MR	magnetic resonance [imaging]
Nuc	nuclear medicine
PA	posteroanterior
PET	positron emission tomography
SBFT	small bowel follow through [barium study]
UGI	upper GI [barium study]
US	ultrasound
V/Q	ventilation perfusion
XR	x-ray

ID/CC	A 54-year-old obese male who is the owner of a chain of fast-food restaurants is brought to the ER after **fainting at work;** earlier in the morning he complained of **dizziness and dyspnea.**
HPI	He had been having episodes of acute, severe, retrosternal chest pain associated with exercise or stress (= ANGINA PECTORIS) for over two years and is taking **propranolol.**
PE	VS: **hypotension (BP 85/60); bradycardia** (52); no fever. PE: patient is conscious; lung fields have **scattered wheezes** (= BRONCHOSPASM); no hepatosplenomegaly or peritoneal signs.
Labs	ECG: QRS normal, but **P-R interval increased** (= FIRST-DEGREE A-V BLOCK). **BUN, ALT** slightly elevated.
Imaging	N/A
Gross Pathology	N/A
Micro Pathology	N/A
Treatment	Treat bradycardia with atropine or isoproterenol. **Bronchospasm** treated with bronchodilators. Treat hypotension with fluids. Glucagon can be life-saving.
Discussion	Used for prevention of angina, as an antihypertensive, in post-MI states, and as an antimigraine agent. Ingestion of 2–3 times the proper dose can be fatal. **Cardiac conduction disturbances** are a common clinical presentation, but severe CNS toxicity, **hypoglycemia** (in diabetics on oral hypoglycemic agents) and hyperkalemia have been reported.

ID/CC   A 62-year-old female is referred to a pulmonary medicine specialist by her family physician because of a **chronic dry cough** that has been **unresponsive to medications.**

HPI   On careful, directed questioning, the specialist discovers that she had been taking **captopril** for hypertension for three years. She also complains of **taste changes** and a **rash** on her chest and lower legs.

PE   VS: normal. PE: no lymphadenopathy; funduscopic exam reveals grade I hypertensive retinopathy; discrete nonpruritic maculopapular **rash** on legs and chest; slight **peripheral edema** (due to persistent proteinuria).

Labs   Serum **renin increased; angiotensin II decreased.** CBC/Lytes/PFTs: normal. SMA-12, liver function tests normal. UA: mild **proteinuria;** normal specific gravity; sediment normal.

Imaging   CXR: no signs of COPD, neoplasm, or other pathology that would account for cough.

Gross Pathology   N/A

Micro Pathology   N/A

Treatment   Usually well tolerated; continue with renal function tests periodically. Consider alternate antihypertensive agents. Aspirin may decrease cough or, alternatively, switch to **losartan.**

Discussion   Captopril is an angiotensin-converting enzyme inhibitor and thus reduces levels of angiotensin II and prevents the inactivation of bradykinin (a potent vasodilator). It is used to treat hypertension, CHF, and diabetic renal disease. It is **contraindicated in pregnancy** because it may cause fetal damage; other side effects are **cough, hypotension, taste changes, rash, proteinuria,** and **angioedema.**

ID/CC   A 74-year-old female who recently had hip replacement surgery has been on **postoperative IV heparin** for five days for the prevention of pulmonary emboli; shortly thereafter, she starts to have black, tarry stools (= MELENA, GI BLEEDING) and to **bleed from the gums** when brushing her teeth

HPI   She suffers from longstanding cardiac disease and has a **history of deep venous thrombosis.** However, the dose administered was excessive.

PE   VS: no fever; **heart rate slightly elevated above baseline;** BP within normal limits but drops when patient stands up (= ORTHOSTATIC HYPOTENSION). PE: **pallor;** no signs or cardiac failure; **incision is oozing blood;** venipuncture sites show large **ecchymoses.**

Labs   CBC: normocytic, normochromic **anemia (7.3mg/dL). Partial thromboplastin time (PTT) markedly elevated; platelet count low;** blood urea nitrogen (BUN) and creatinine elevated.

Imaging   CXR: within normal limits for age. XR - Hip: no evidence of hematoma formation.

Gross Pathology   N/A

Micro Pathology   N/A

Treatment   In heparin overdosage, slow IV **protamine** is the specific antidote.

Discussion   Heparin catalyzes the **antithrombin-protease reaction,** thereby enhancing the anticlotting effects of antithrombin. Its major adverse effect is bleeding, and careful control of the dose is essential. Patients with renal failure are more prone to hemorrhage. Heparin can also cause a transient thrombocytopenia in ~25% of patients. Protamine is a cationic protein that rapidly binds and inactivates heparin. The onset of action is nearly immediate.

ID/CC   A 45-year-old female news reporter is brought to the ER from work after she was noted to be **disoriented;** she also complained of a **splitting headache** and **ringing in her ears.**

HPI   She **vomited** twice while in the ambulance. Paramedics noticed a MedicAlert bracelet stating that she has **Graves' disease** (susceptibility to hypertensive crises).

PE   VS: **hypertension** (BP 190/120). PE: diffuse **alteration in mental status** (hypertensive encephalopathy); **retinal hemorrhages** bilaterally on funduscopic exam; patient could not lift left heel off examining table (focal neurologic deficit); chest and abdominal exam normal; femoral pulses palpable (vs. aortic coarctation, another cause of hypertensive crisis).

Labs   Hyperglycemia (147 mg/dL); creatine kinase, LDH, AST, and ALT normal; no increase in vanillylmandelic acid (vs. pheochromocytoma). UA: proteinuria. ECG: no evidence of MI.

Imaging   CT/MR - Head: no intracranial mass or evidence of hemorrhage found.

Gross Pathology   N/A

Micro Pathology   N/A

Treatment   Do not attempt to lower BP more than 30% in the first hour due to possible coma or MI. Treatment with intensive care, surveillance of vital signs and progress.

Discussion   Nitroprusside (potent arteriolar and venular vasodilator) reduces preload and afterload and has very rapid onset and end of action (easy titration in case of hypertensive emergencies), making it the first drug of choice. It requires constant surveillance, however, and may produce cyanide toxicity (arrhythmias, hallucinations, acidosis, psychosis). Nicardipine, labetalol, and phentolamine (specifically for pheochromocytoma) are other common drug alternatives.

ID/CC An anesthesiologist is summoned into the OR when a 34-year-old male undergoing a **routine hernia repair** begins to have **seizures.**

HPI The surgeon was chatting with the chief resident while injecting **lidocaine** subcutaneously for a local anesthetic repair when the patient started having slurred speech, tremors, and then **tonic-clonic convulsions** (lidocaine was inadvertently injected systemically into the inferior epigastric vessels).

PE Lips and fingertips blue (= CYANOSIS); patient **biting his tongue;** blood oozing from mouth; eyes rolled inward; extremities and spine in spastic state with shaking movements at intervals.

Labs There was no time to take blood samples, and treatment was initiated.

Imaging N/A

Gross Pathology N/A

Micro Pathology N/A

Treatment Control seizures if patient has a line with diazepam or barbiturates. Intubate, oxygenate, and ventilate in anticipation of second phase (respiratory depression).

Discussion Lidocaine, the most widely used local anesthetic, is an amide that blocks sodium channels by binding to specific receptors. Overdosage follows inadvertent systemic injection, mainly in obstetric and surgical procedures, and is manifested by CNS toxicity (seizures) and a "hyper" state **followed by a depressive period** with hypothermia, hypotension, and cardiorespiratory depression. Toxicity should be differentiated from the rare anaphylactic reaction and the commonplace anxiety-induced vasovagal syncope or epinephrine-induced anxiety (lidocaine is often injected together with epinephrine in order to increase the period of effectiveness via vasoconstriction and decreased lidocaine absorption).

MAO Inhibitor Hypertensive Crisis

ID/CC A 43-year-old art consultant in an advertising agency is brought to the emergency room with **severe headache, ringing in her ears, and dizziness;** she had been **drinking** and dining together at a French restaurant.

HPI Over the past several months she had seen several physicians for a variety of complaints before finally being diagnosed with **hypochondriasis** and given medication for it **(tranylcypromine).**

PE VS: tachycardia; **hypertension** (BP 180/120); no fever. PE: no papilledema; no signs of longstanding hypertensive retinopathy; no goiter (hyperthyroidism may lead to hypertensive crises); radial and femoral pulses felt normally (vs. coarctation of aorta).

Labs CBC/Lytes: normal. Liver function tests normal; no vanillylmandelic acid in urine (seen in pheochromocytoma). UA: normal.

Imaging CXR: normal.

Gross Pathology N/A

Micro Pathology N/A

Treatment Gastric lavage, activated charcoal, treat hypertensive crisis. Avoid tyramine-containing foods.

Discussion Monoamine oxidase (MAO) is an enzyme that degrades catecholamines. When inhibited, catecholamine and serotonin levels increase. MAO inhibitors, such **as tranylcypromine, isocarboxazid,** and **phenelzine** are used to treat **anxiety, hypochondriasis,** and **atypical depressions. Tyramine** is a catecholamine food precursor found in **fermented cheese and red wine.** When taken together, tyramine and MAO inhibitors rapidly elevate blood pressure with possible encephalopathy and stroke. **Profound hypotension** may occur as well as refractory **hyperthermia.**

ID/CC	A 52-year-old man visits his physician complaining of **extreme tiredness, dry mouth, and easy fatigability;** he states that he has never experienced symptoms like these before.
HPI	He was started on hydrochlorothiazide for treatment of hypertension, but it did not control his hypertension, so **alpha-methyldopa** was added approximately two months ago. On directed questioning, he states that he has been suffering from **sexual dysfunction** (impotence and inability to ejaculate) for the past several weeks.
PE	VS: BP 130/90, but when standing up it is 100/60 (= ORTHOSTATIC HYPOTENSION); no fever; bradycardia (58). PE: **conjunctival pallor;** patient oriented with regard to person, time, and place; well hydrated despite **dryness of mouth;** funduscopic exam normal; no neck masses or bruits; no lymphadenopathy; chest auscultation normal; abdomen soft and nontender with no masses; no peritoneal signs.
Labs	CBC: **positive Coombs' test;** decreased hemoglobin and hematocrit; **increased reticulocytes; decreased haptoglobin.** UA: hemoglobinuria. Increased indirect bilirubin; normal iron levels; **AST and ALT moderately increased.**
Imaging	CXR/KUB: normal for age.
Gross Pathology	N/A
Micro Pathology	N/A
Treatment	Switch antihypertensive treatment.
Discussion	Methyldopa is a sympatholytic that produces a false neurotransmitter, alpha-methyl-norepinephrine. It is used as an antihypertensive drug, and its side effects include impotence, Coombs positivity and, more rarely hemolytic anemia. It can also cause sedation and drowsiness, along with severe orthostatic hypotension.

ID/CC The 48-year-old chief executive officer of a leading auto manufacturer is put on **niacin** and a restricted diet for the treatment of **high-LDL cholesterol.**

HPI The patient is a "bon vivant" who enjoys **drinking** and **eating** gourmet food as well as **smoking** two packs a day of Cuban filter-free dark tobacco cigarettes. On a visit two months afterward, the patient's lab tests show improvement, but he complains of **facial flushing** and **itching** on the lower back, palms, and anus.

PE VS: mild hypertension (BP 145/95). PE: obesity; facial redness; no skin rash demonstrable on inspection.

Labs **Serum glucose elevated (157mg/dL);** LDL lowered considerably in comparison to last visit; triglycerides decreased, but not as markedly; HDL increased; **AST and ALT** mildly **elevated; normal** levels of 5-hydroxyindoleacetic acid (vs. carcinoid syndrome which may also produce facial flushing).

Imaging CXR: normal.

Gross Pathology N/A

Micro Pathology N/A

Treatment Prostaglandin inhibitors.

Discussion Nicotinic acid (= NIACIN) is a derivative of tryptophan, a constituent of NAD and NADP that is used in redox reactions. As a drug, it is used for its lipid-lowering properties (decreases VLDL, decreases LDL, and increases HDL cholesterol). Its main side effects, **flushing** and **pruritus,** seem to be **mediated by prostaglandins** and thus are **reduced by aspirin and NSAIDs. Hepatitis, hyperglycemia,** and exacerbation of peptic ulcer are other side effects.

ID/CC	A 53-year-old male **chemical-factory worker** presents with **chronic headaches and dizziness** with occasional **chest pain.**
HPI	The patient states that his headaches and dizziness occur most frequently when he **returns to work** after a few days off; he is otherwise in good health.
PE	VS: mild hypertension. PE: patient appears normal but **slightly cyanotic;** neck exam shows no masses or carotid bruit; cardiac exam normal; lungs fields clear; abdomen soft and nontender; no hepatosplenomegaly; no focal neurologic signs.
Labs	CBC: normal; SMA-7 normal. UA: normal. **Methemoglobin levels elevated.** ECG: no sign of ischemia or necrosis.
Imaging	CXR/KUB: within normal limits for age.
Gross Pathology	N/A
Micro Pathology	N/A
Treatment	Hemodialysis and hemoperfusion are not effective in chronic nitrate exposure; monitor vital signs.
Discussion	Nitrates are a large class of drugs which are used in treatment of angina. All agents in this group, including nitroglycerin, act through nitric oxide (NO) release. NO, in turn, is a potent vasodilator of vascular smooth muscle. These compounds have a short half-life and may **produce tolerance in chronically exposed individuals.** Patients may suffer **angina or MI** as a result of **rebound** coronary **vasoconstriction** due to withdrawal.

ID/CC   A 58-year-old man comes to see his cardiologist because of an **increased need for nitroglycerin patches** in order to control his oppressive exercise-induced chest pain (= ANGINA).

HPI   In the past, taking one tablet five minutes before physical activity controlled his symptoms; now he has to take two tablets. The patient has continued to smoke two packs of cigarettes each day and is concerned that his cardiac condition is worsening because of this **increased need for medication.**

PE   VS: normotension. PE: obese male in no acute distress; no rales or crackles on lungs fields; heart sounds normal; no murmurs; no third or fourth heart sounds; fingertips cigarette-stained; no hepatosplenomegaly; no increase in jugular venous pressure; no leg edema.

Labs   CBC: elevated hematocrit. Elevated glucose (154 mg/dL); **hypercholesterolemia; hypertriglyceridemia;** blood urea nitrogen (BUN) and creatinine normal; liver function tests normal. ECG: no signs of ischemia or infarction.

Imaging   CXR: calcification of aortic knob, left ventricular hypertrophy. Echo: no segmental wall abnormalities.

Gross Pathology   Atherosclerotic narrowing of coronary arteries.

Micro Pathology   N/A

Treatment   Adjust timing of nitrate administration in order to have an eight-hour period free of nitroglycerin. Consider beta blockers and calcium channel blocking agents.

Discussion   Together with **pulsating headache,** the need to **progressively increase the dosage of the drug** (= TOLERANCE) is the **main drawback of nitrate use** for treatment of angina. Nitrates produce vasodilation of arterioles and venules, thereby reducing both preload and afterload work of the heart.

ID/CC   A 56-year-old male comes to the cardiology unit for evaluation of **ringing in his ears** (= TINNITUS), **dizziness, GI distress** (= NAUSEA, VOMITING AND DIARRHEA), and **headaches**.

HPI   He also complains of **blurred vision** and **impaired hearing**. The patient had an MI one year ago and has been receiving oral **quinidine** antiarrhythmic therapy.

PE   VS: **bradycardia** (55); normotension (110/70). PE: eye mechanism of **accommodation impaired** but funduscopic exam normal; **skin flushed** and sweaty; hands show fine **tremors;** no heart murmurs; lungs clear; abdomen soft, nontender, and free of masses; no peritoneal signs; bowel sounds hyperactive.

Labs   CBC: normal. Lytes: normal. ECG: **prolonged QRS and Q-T intervals.**

Imaging   CXR: no pulmonary edema.

Gross Pathology   N/A

Micro Pathology   N/A

Treatment   Monitor ECG and vital signs. Treat cardiotoxic effects with hypertonic sodium bicarbonate to reverse ECG changes and hypotension. Change to different antiarrhythmic drug.

Discussion   Quinidine, procainamide, and disopyramide are type IA antiarrhythmics that act by blocking sodium channels, increasing the effective refractory period. They are used for both atrial and ventricular arrhythmias. All these agents have low therapeutic-toxic ratios and may produce severe adverse reactions. Cinchonism is the state commonly produced by drugs such as quinidine, quinine and chloroquine with signs and symptoms as in this case. Other quinidine side effects may include xerostomia and mydriasis as well as CNS signs such as **delirium.**

ID/CC   A 76-year-old female comes to her family doctor complaining of **constipation** and epigastric pain as well as **weakness** and painful **muscle cramps** (due to hypokalemia).

HPI   She has a history of hypertension, for which she has been taking propranolol and **hydrochlorothiazide** for the past several months.

PE   VS: mild hypertension (145/90); no fever. PE: well hydrated; funduscopic exam shows **hypertensive retinopathy grade II**; no increase in jugular venous pressure; no masses in neck; no carotid bruit; soft third heart sound; no hepatomegaly; no pitting edema of lower legs; **deep tendon reflexes hypoactive** (hypokalemia).

Labs   Increased hematocrit (hemoconcentration); increase in blood urea nitrogen (BUN); **hyperglycemia.** Lytes: **hypokalemia; hyponatremia. Hyperlipidemia; hyperuricemia.** UA: proteinuria; high specific gravity. ABGs: **metabolic alkalosis.** ECG: S-T segment and T-wave depression; U waves (due to hypokalemia); shortened Q-T (due to hypercalcemia).

Imaging   N/A

Gross Pathology   N/A

Micro Pathology   N/A

Treatment   Potassium-rich foods (chickpeas, bananas, papaya), potassium supplement, or switch to potassium-sparing diuretics such as spironolactone and triamterene.

Discussion   Thiazides, the most commonly used diuretics (of which hydrochlorothiazide is the prototype), are sulfonamides that act by inhibiting sodium chloride reabsorption in the distal tubule. They are used mainly in congestive heart failure, edematous states, and hypertension (they have a mild vasodilating effect). The hyperuricemia induced by thiazide diuretics can also precipiate bouts of **gout.**

ID/CC   A 73-year-old white widow visits her cardiologist complaining of **difficulty moving her bowels** for the past week; she also reports **facial flushing.**

HPI   She had been regular until she began taking **verapamil** for an irregular heart beat one month ago.

PE   VS: hear rate normal; normotension; no fever. PE: in no acute distress; left eye cataract, no pallor, no neck masses, no lymphadenopathy, lungs clear; cardiac exam normal; abdomen soft, nondistended; no palpable masses; no peritoneal signs; mild lower leg **edema.**

Labs   CBC/Lytes/UA: normal. Blood urea nitrogen (BUN), glucose, liver function tests normal; no hypercalcemia (may produce constipation); normal levels of 5-hydroxyindoleacetic acid (vs. carcinoid syndrome which may also produce facial flushing but not constipation).

Imaging   CXR: within normal limits for age. KUB: moderate degree of osteoporosis as well as arthritic changes in lumbar spine.

Gross Pathology   N/A

Micro Pathology   N/A

Treatment   Increase fluids in diet, regular exercise, fruits, high-bulk foods, or **bulk laxatives.** If persistent, change to another calcium channel blocker.

Discussion   Verapamil is one of the agents that block voltage-dependent calcium channels, consequently reducing muscle contractility. Verapamil acts more specifically on myocardial fibers than on arteriolar smooth muscle. It is widely used as an antihypertensive, as an antiarrhythmic agent, and for treatment of angina pectoris. **Constipation** is a common side effect, as are dizziness, facial **flushing** and peripheral edema.

14　Stevens-Johnson Syndrome

ID/CC　A 19-year-old female is admitted to the internal medicine ward because of **generalized desquamation** of the skin, high **fever,** and painful **ulcers and bullae in her eyes and vagina.**

HPI　She adds that **swallowing** is extremely **painful** and that **her gums bleed** with minor trauma. She denies any history of allergies. For the past week, she has been on oral **sulfonamides** for a urinary tract infection.

PE　VS: **fever** (39.2 C). PE: patient in acute distress; pain in all areas of **ulceration,** including conjunctiva, nasal mucosa, mouth, oropharynx, and vagina; eyelids swollen and erythematous; **generalized, symmetric rash** on skin with **macules, papules, vesicles,** and **bullae** (multiple primary skin lesions) as well as areas of denudation (epidermis completely separated from dermis) on palms, soles, and extremities.

Labs　Biopsy distinguishes from toxic epidermal necrolysis, pemphigus, and pemphigoid.

Imaging　N/A

Gross Pathology　N/A

Micro Pathology　Dermal edema with perivascular inflammatory infiltrate and epidermal separation in bullae showing necrotic and hemorrhagic areas.

Treatment　Hospitalization, discontinue sulfa drug, IV steroids, local lidocaine.

Discussion　Also called **erythema multiforme major.** Grave, acute, sometimes fatal disease with generalized skin **desquamation** and severe **ulcers and bullae** on at least two mucosal surfaces, including genitalia, mouth, conjunctiva, nose, or lips. Use of sulfa drugs (bacteriostatic antibiotics which are PABA antimetabolites that inhibit dihydropteroate synthase) is the a common precipitating factor. Other drugs implicated are phenytoin and NSAIDs.

ID/CC   A 19-year-old **red-haired** female visits her dermatologist at a local clinic because of a **rash** that appeared after she spent the sunny weekend hiking without sun block protection.

HPI   Two months ago, her dermatologist put her on low-dose **tetracycline** to prevent acne flare-ups.

PE   VS: normal. PE: patient **blue-eyed** and **fair-skinned;** red, nonpruritic, **maculopapular rash** that blanches on pressure on "V" of the anterior neck, posterior neck, forearms, hands, and face, sparing rest of body (rash is on sun-exposed areas of body); chest, abdomen, and neuro exams fail to disclose pathology.

Labs   Pregnancy test negative. CBC/Lytes: normal. Liver function tests within normal limits. UA: mild **proteinuria.**

Imaging   N/A

Gross Pathology   N/A

Micro Pathology   N/A

Treatment   Sun protection, both mechanical and pharmacologic, while taking tetracycline.

Discussion   Tetracyclines are bacteriostatic antibiotics than bind to the 30S ribosomal unit, blocking synthesis of protein by preventing attachment of aminoacyl-tRNA. If taken with alkaline foods such as milk and antacids, GI absorption is decreased. Tetracycline is used both therapeutically and prophylactically for chlamydial genitourinary infections, Lyme disease, tularemia, cholera, and acne. Untoward effects include **brownish discoloration of teeth in children** (contraindicated in pregnancy), photosensitivity, aminoaciduria, proteinuria, phosphaturia, acidosis, and glycosuria (Fanconi-like syndrome).

ID/CC   A 26-year-old obsessive-compulsive female comes to the family medicine clinic to have her 5-year-old daughter checked by a dermatologist because of **itching and scaling of her skin.**

HPI   The mother is very thin and fears that her daughter will not gain enough weight, so she has given her **cod-liver oil** (rich in vitamin A) **four times a day for the past nine months.** The child complains of **fatigue and headaches.**

PE   Funduscopic exam: **papilledema** (pseudotumor cerebri). localized areas of hair loss (= ALOPECIA); very **dry skin** with **scaling** areas on back and extremities; **liver** moderately **enlarged** but not painful; **hyperkeratosis** on medial side of soles of feet.

Labs   Increased levels of vitamin A in serum.

Imaging   XR - Long Bones and Spine: **subcortical hyperostosis.**

Gross Pathology   N/A

Micro Pathology   N/A

Treatment   Avoidance of vitamin A-containing oil.

Discussion   Together with vitamins D, E, and K, vitamin A is one of the fat-soluble vitamins, which means that the body stores them and does not eliminate them as quickly as water-soluble vitamins. Vitamin A (= RETINOL) is derived from carotenes and is a constituent of retinal pigments (= RHODOPSIN). Vitamin A is necessary for the integrity of all epithelial cells. **Lack of vitamin A** produces **night blindness** and **xerophthalmia.**

ID/CC A 32-year-old male, a professional weight lifter, comes to the family medicine clinic for evaluation of **impotence** for the past four months.

HPI His girlfriend reports increasingly **aggressive** and **labile behavior.** He has a history of multiple cycles of oral and injectable **anabolic steroid abuse.**

PE VS: **borderline hypertension.** PE: young, muscular male; androgenic **alopecia; acne; testicular atrophy.**

Labs CBC/Lytes: normal. AST, ALT normal; **hyperglycemia** (145 mg/dL). BUN (blood urea nitrogen) and creatinine normal. Decreased HDL-C levels. **Oligospermia** on semen analysis.

Imaging CXR: normal. XR - Long Bones and Spine: normal calcification.

Gross Pathology N/A

Micro Pathology N/A

Treatment Discontinue androgens.

Discussion Anabolic steroids are widely abused by weight lifters, other athletes, and the lay public. Although androgens increase muscle mass significantly, they produce only slight increases in strength. Numerous side effects have been reported, including **hepatic neoplasia, glucose intolerance, decreased HDL-C levels, hypertension, testicular atrophy and oligospermia, virilization** and amenorrhea, **acne,** and **alopecia.** Other consequences of androgen abuse include mood disturbances and **irritability** that may result in **aggressive behavior** and injury to others.

ID/CC   A 32-year-old woman comes to her first ever gynecologic visit.

HPI   On routine pelvic exam a vaginal **mass** is felt. On directed questioning, it was clear that the **patient's mother took an estrogen compound** (DES) during pregnancy as treatment for threatened abortion.

PE   VS: normal. PE: well developed with breast tissue according to age; pubic and axillary hair normal; on bimanual pelvic examination a **hard, ulcerated mass** is felt on the posterior **wall of upper vagina**; iodine staining of vaginal wall shows patches of decreased uptake by cells (adenosis).

Labs   CBC/Lytes/UA: normal. Hormonal screen and liver function tests do not disclose any abnormality.

Imaging   Hysterosalpingogram: injection of contrast into uterine cavity reveals T-shaped uterus and cervical incompetence.

Gross Pathology   N/A

Micro Pathology   Biopsy by colposcopy shows glandular epithelium in upper part of vagina with squamous metaplasia (ADENOSIS). Biopsy of the ulcerated mass shows clear-cell adenocarcinoma of vagina.

Treatment   Surgery; radiation.

Discussion   Diethylstilbestrol is a synthetic estrogen that was used some 30-35 years ago for threatened abortion. The daughters of patients thus treated before the 18th week of pregnancy may present an alteration in the development of the embryonic transition between the urogenital canal and paramesonephric system, producing persistence of mullerian glands on upper vagina, giving rise to adenosis and clear cell adenocarcinoma that is usually asymptomatic and discovered incidentally. Other side effects include transverse vaginal septum, developmental uterine abnormalities, and cervical incompetence.

ID/CC A 46-year-old female comes to the medical clinic for an evaluation of **weight gain, roundness of her face,** and epigastric pain that is relieved by eating (peptic ulcer).

HPI She had been suffering from chronic, itchy blisters in the mouth that came and went leaving painful ulcers, together with large bullae on all four extremities, chest, and lower back (= PEMPHIGUS), for which she has been taking **high-dose prednisone** for several months.

PE VS: hypertension (BP 145/95); no fever. PE: patient has **moon facies, a buffalo hump,** and **obesity of the truncal type;** muscle wasting and increased facial hair.

Labs CBC: leukocytosis with **lymphopenia. Hyperglycemia.** Lytes: **hypokalemia.** UA: glycosuria.

Imaging XR - Spine and Long Bones: generalized **osteoporosis.**

Gross Pathology N/A

Micro Pathology N/A

Treatment Switch to methotrexate, azathioprine, dapsone, or nicotinamide. Corticosteroids should be tapered down.

Discussion Of the causes of Cushing's syndrome, iatrogenesis is the most common. Steroids produce a lysosomal membrane stabilization, blocking leukotriene formation from arachidonic acid, blocking the action of phospholipase A, and inhibiting cyclooxygenase activity (decreased prostaglandin formation). Because of this, they are utilized in a number of settings, such as acute inflammation, anaphylaxis, allergy states, and immune suppression as well as for the treatment of Addison's disease.

ID/CC   A 17-year-old white female student who is learning how to inject herself **insulin** is found **unconscious** by her desk.

HPI   The patient suffered from weight loss, polyuria, polydipsia, and polyphagia for several months and was recently diagnosed with **juvenile-onset diabetes mellitus**. She has been meticulous in self-administering her insulin injections and often inject larger doses of insulin than prescribed (overdosages are usual at the beggining of treatment).

PE   VS: **tachycardia** (96), **hypotension** (100/50), no fever. PE: **skin cold and moist**, patient **stuporous** with hyporeflexia; negative Babinski's sign; responsive only to painful stimuli; cardiopulmonary exam normal; no hepatomegaly; no splenomegaly; no peritoneal signs.

Labs   **Severely hypoglycemic.** Lytes: potassium and magnesium levels sharply decreased (HYPOKALEMIA, HYPOMAGNASEMIA). BUN and creatinine normal.

Imaging   CT - Head: no intracranial pathology demonstrated to account for the stuporous state.

Gross Pathology   N/A

Micro Pathology   N/A

Treatment Administer 50% glucose after drawing baseline blood sample. Follow serum glucose levels for several hours, monitor and treat electrolyte inbalances.

Discussion With the administration of insulin, blood glucose levels are lowered by direct stimulation of cellular uptake. Glucose uptake is accompanied by a shift of magnesium and potassium into the cell. A severe hypoglycemic coma may result from an insulin overdose, which can produce **permanent neurologic damage or death**.

ID/CC A 36-year-old female oboe player is brought by ambulance to the emergency room because of gradual numbness and **weakness on the left side of her face and arm** together with **headache** and dizziness.

HPI She is **obese** and **smokes** one pack of cigarettes a day. She is currently taking **oral contraceptive pills** (OCPs).

PE VS: normal. PE: patient conscious, oriented, and able to speak; **gaze is deviated to the right;** funduscopic exam does not show papilledema, hypertension, or diabetic retinopathy; lungs clear; abdomen soft and nontender; no peritoneal signs; **left arm and leg weakness with hyporeflexia.**

Labs CBC/Lytes: normal. **Hyperlipidemia; hyperglycemia;** blood urea nitrogen (BUN) and creatinine normal; RPR negative; protein C and protein S negative. ECG: normal.

Imaging CT - Head: negative. Arteriography: thrombotic cerebral arterial occlusion.

Gross Pathology N/A

Micro Pathology N/A

Treatment Intensive care treatment and surveillance for stroke in evolution. Evaluate anticoagulation, discontinue OCPs.

Discussion Oral contraceptive pills are a very popular method of birth control. There are many OCP preparations, most of which consist of a combination of estrogens and progestins, which, when taken daily, selectively inhibits pituitary function to prevent ovulation. The most severe complication is an **increased incidence of vascular thrombotic events,** either cerebral or myocardial. Other side effects include nausea, acne, weight gain, psychological depression, cholestatic jaundice, increased incidence of vaginal infections, headaches, and breakthrough bleeding. They should be used cautiously in patients with asthma, diabetes, liver disease, and hypertension.

Drug-Induced Hemorrhagic Gastritis

ID/CC A 58-year-old female comes to the emergency room because of acute, burning **epigastric pain** accompanied by nausea and **vomiting** of **bright red blood.**

HPI She is a chronic sufferer of rheumatoid arthritis and has taken 650 mg of **aspirin** every 8 hours for her pain for the past four years to control her pain.

PE VS: **tachycardia** (98); hypotension (BP 110/60); no fever. PE: **pallor;** anxiety; abdomen shows **tenderness on deep palpation in epigastrium;** no rigidity, guarding, or rebound tenderness; no masses palpable; no focal neurologic signs; hands show characteristic rheumatoid characteristics.

Labs CBC: Hb and hematocrit low. ABGs/Lytes: mild metabolic alkalosis with hypokalemia (due to vomiting of hydrochloric acid).

Imaging Endoscopy: gastric mucosa markedly hyperemic with hemorrhagic spotting and zones of recent hemorrhage; no ulcer or tumor observed.

Gross Pathology N/A

Micro Pathology N/A

Treatment Discontinue offending agent (salicylates); start mucosal protectors, antacids, proton pump inhibitors, or H_2 receptor blockers.

Discussion Hemorrhagic gastritis is seen in individuals who take drugs that may cause damage to the mucosa, such as aspirin, NSAIDs, steroids, and alcohol. Critically ill patients, such as those with burns, sepsis, cranial trauma, and coagulation defects, may also bleed from the stomach. Acetylsalicylic acid (aspirin) acetylates and irreversibly inhibits cyclooxygenase I and II to prevent conversion of arachidonic acid to prostaglandins.

ID/CC	A 39-year-old male presents to his family doctor because of increasing embarrassment and concern over **breast enlargement**.
HPI	The patient has a long history of burning epigastric pain on awakening in the mornings and in between meals that decreased with food and antacids (peptic ulcer disease), for which he had been taking **cimetidine**. Directed questioning reveals that he also suffers from **impotence**.
PE	VS: normal. PE: cardiovascular, neurologic, and abdominal examination fail to reveal any pathology; moderate growth of breast tissue bilaterally; few drops of whitish secretion expressed from nipple (GALACTORRHEA); **testes** somewhat **hypotrophic**; rectal exam negative for prostatic enlargement.
Labs	CBC/Lytes/UA: normal. **AST and ALT** mildly **elevated; alkaline phosphatase and creatinine mildly elevated.** BUN (blood urea nitrogen) normal.
Imaging	CXR/KUB: normal.
Gross Pathology	N/A
Micro Pathology	N/A
Treatment	Switch to other histamine receptor antagonists such as ranitidine or famotidine.
Discussion	All the H_2 blockers are well tolerated, although cimetidine is associated with several side effects, particularly **reversible gynecomastia**. Cimetidine produces an **increase in serum prolactin levels** and alters estrogen metabolism in men (has antiadrogenic properties). Other side effects include headache, confusion, low sperm counts, and hematologic abnormalities (may enhance hypoprotrombinemic effect of oral anticoagulants). It has been largeley supplanted by newer H_2 receptor blockers without these side effects.

ID/CC A 64-year-old female is brought to the emergency room because of the development of high fever, **marked jaundice**, weakness, profound fatigue, and **darkening of her urine.**

HPI She has undergone different many surgical procedures **under general anesthesia** (halothane) over the past two years including a colpoperineoplasty, an endometrial biopsy, a femoral hernia repair, and, four weeks ago, a total hip replacement. After each surgery, the patient developed a low-grade fever within a few days.

PE VS: **tachycardia** (93), hypotension (100/55), fever (39.2). PE: **marked weakness**; diaphoresis; patients appears **toxic**; profound **jaundice** in mucosal membranes; liver edge palpable 3 cm below costal margin; liver tenderness.

Labs CBC: marked **leukocytosis** (18,500), with **eosinophilia** (18%) (allergic reaction). Hypoglycemia; **AST and ALT markedly elevated; elevated alkaline phosphatase and bilirubin.**

Imaging N/A

Gross Pathology Massive centrolobular hepatic necrosis with fatty change.

Micro Pathology N/A

Treatment Monitor liver function and assess bilirubin and glucose levels and prothrombin time. Provide intensive supportive care for possible hepatic failure and encephalopathy. Glucose, fresh-frozen plasma, and lactulose.

Discussion All inhaled anesthetics cause a decrease in hepatic blood flow, but rarely will this result in permanent changes in liver function tests. Nevertheless, **halocarbon drugs,** which include halothane (2-BROMO, 2-CHLORO TRIFLUOROETHANE), are considered to be **hepatotoxins** and very rarely may produce postoperative jaundice, massive hepatic necrosis, and death. Fulminant post-halothane hepatic necrosis normally occurs 4—6 weeks after the insult.

ID/CC	A 52-year-old HIV-positive male who was diagnosed with **tuberculosis** eight months ago and was started on **isoniazid** therapy presents with **jaundice**.
HPI	The patient's isoniazid therapy was uneventful until two weeks ago, when he began to appear jaundiced. He also complains of **lack of strength in his left foot**.
PE	VS: normal. PE: patient appears lethargic; yellowed sclera and discoloration of skin; funduscopic exam normal; moderate, nontender hepatomegaly; left foot drop (peroneal nerve involvement); no lymphadenopathy; splenomegaly.
Labs	Moderately increased AST, ALT, bilirubin, DHL, alkaline phosphatase, and gamma glutamyl transferase.
Imaging	US: shows generalized mild enlargement of liver with no focal lesions.
Gross Pathology	N/A
Micro Pathology	N/A
Treatment	Supportive measures Pyridoxine treatment may be ameliorative in some cases.
Discussion	Isoniazid (ISONICOTINIC ACID HYDRAZIDE) decreases the synthesis of mycolic acids and is the bactericidal drug of choice for tuberculous prophylaxis. It is used as combination therapy for erradication of *Mycobacterium tuberculosis*. Chronic use is associated with hepatitis, peripheral neuritis, and systemic lupus erythematosus. INH competes with pyridoxine for the enzyme apotryptophanase, thus producing a deficiency of pyridoxine. The administration of pyridoxine can prevent some central and peripheral nervous system effects. The risk for hepatitis and multilobular necrosis is greater in alcoholics and older persons.

ID/CC A 38-year-old male complains of **burning epigastric pain** that **awakens him at night** together with nausea and vomiting.

HPI He states that he has experienced this pain **on and off** for several months and that it used to **disappear with food** consumption but now persists.

PE VS: normal. PE: mild epigastric tenderness on deep palpation without peritoneal signs; no pathologic signs found; physical exam otherwise unremarkable.

Labs CBC/Lytes/UA: normal. Stool ova and parasites negative; guaiac test negative (no occult blood in feces); **breath ammonia test positive** (*Helicobacter pylori*).

Imaging UGI and barium series from six months ago showed no apparent pathology. Endoscopy: chronic gastritis and **duodenal ulcer.** A biopsy is taken.

Gross Pathology N/A

Micro Pathology Acute and chronic inflammatory infiltrate with no cellular atypia on biopsy; positive for *Helicobacter pylori*.

Treatment Diet; exercise; stress reduction; small frequent meals; *H. pylori* eradication (through one of several combination drug regimens that include bismuth, amoxicillin, tetracycline, metronidazole, clarithromycin, and omeprazole).

Discussion Drugs such as ranitidine and famotidine are histamine analogs that reversibly block H_2 receptor blockers, thereby inhibiting the effect of histamine on gastric secretion. They are extremely popular and are the cause of a dramatic decrease in the number of operable complications of peptic ulcer disease (perforation, penetration, obstruction, bleeding). Drugs such as omeprazole (a proton pump inhibitor), which act by inhibiting H^+/K^+-ATPase in the parietal cells of the stomach, have also contributed greatly to this trend. They are particularly useful in Zollinger–Ellison syndrome. The role of *H. pylori* in the pathogenesis of peptic ulcer disease is increasingly being recognized.

Pseudomembranous Enterocolitis

ID/CC A 28-year-old white female has surgery due to perforated appendicitis with peritonitis; 10 days postoperatively she develops fever, abdominal cramping, and **watery diarrhea with pus and mucus.**

HPI Her postoperative recovery was unremarkable until the onset of diarrhea. She had **received continuous parenteral antibiotics** (clindamycin).

PE VS: fever; tachycardia; tachypnea. PE: moderate dehydration; mild abdominal tenderness with no signs of peritoneal irritation; surgical wound normal.

Labs CBC: leukocytosis. Stool culture reveals gram-positive cocci, *Clostridium difficile*; **presence of toxin in stool.**

Imaging Sigmoidoscopy: mucosal hyperemia, ulcers, and **pseudomembranes.**

Gross Pathology Mucosa hyperemic and swollen; epithelial ulcerations covered by yellowish plaques (pseudomembranes) and fibrinous exudate.

Micro Pathology Fibrinous exudate with pseudomembrane formation; ulceration of superficial epithelium; neutrophilic infiltrate with necrotic debris.

Treatment Cessation of offending antibiotic; give **metronidazole** or oral vancomycin.

Discussion Acute inflammation of colon in patients taking antibiotics, specifically **clindamycin** or ampicillin, due to **overgrowth of *C. difficile*;** characterized by formation of **pseudomembranes.** Clindamycin acts by blocking protein synthesis at the 50S ribosomal unit. Its main clinical indication is for life-threatening infections with **anaerobes.**

Aflatoxin Carcinogenicity

ID/CC A 61-year-old male is admitted to the internal medicine ward for evaluation of **weight loss** and an **increase in abdominal girth.**

HPI He is the father of an African student who is currently studying in the U.S. His son brought him here from Central **Africa** for treatment of his disease.

PE Thin, emaciated male; marked **jaundice;** abdomen markedly enlarged due to **ascitic fluid; hepatomegaly;** pitting **edema** in both lower legs.

Labs CBC: anemia (Hb 6.3) (sometimes there might be polycythemia due to ectopic erythropoietin secretion). **Increased alpha-fetoprotein; hypoglycemia** (due to increased glycogen storage); AST and ALT elevated; alkaline phosphatase elevated.

Imaging US/CT - Abdomen: enlargement of liver with multiple nodularities involving the vena cava; enlargement of regional lymph nodes.

Gross Pathology N/A

Micro Pathology Liver biopsy confirms clinical diagnosis, showing fibrotic changes and glycogen accumulation with vacuolation and multinucleated giant cells; pleomorphic hepatocytes in a trabecular pattern (may also be adenoid or anaplastic) with malignant change (hepatocellular carcinoma).

Treatment Palliative.

Discussion Hepatocellular carcinoma is frequently seen in association with hepatitis B virus infections and with cirrhosis. There is a dramatic predisposition to this neoplasia in Africa and in parts of Asia and is the most common visceral neoplasia in African men. Causative theories include the carcinogenic action of aflatoxins on genetically susceptible individuals. Aflatoxins are produced by the contamination of peanuts (staple food in many African countries) by the fungus *Aspergillus favus.*

ID/CC　During ward rounds, a 28-year-old HIV-positive female patient complains that after a period of improvement since her admission three days ago, she now feels very sick, with **palpitations, high fever, and marked lightheadedness.**

HPI　She was admitted because of **cryptococcal meningitis** and was started on **amphotericin B.**

PE　VS: tachycardia (93); **hypotension** (BP 90/55); fever (39.3 C). PE: mild dyspnea; disseminated rales in both lung fields; heart sounds show **skipped beats;** nuchal rigidity resolved; mental status improved; pitting **edema** on both lower legs.

Labs　CBC: mild anemia; normal leukocytes. **BUN and creatinine** moderately **elevated;** positive capsular cryptococcal serum antigen. LP: still increased protein and decreased glucose in CSF, but improved since admission.

Imaging　CXR: discrete bilateral pulmonary infiltrates, predominantly in perihilar areas.

Gross Pathology　N/A

Micro Pathology　N/A

Treatment　Lower dosage of amphotericin B or change to oral fluconazole.

Discussion　Mechanism of action of amphotericin B is by **binding to ergosterol in fungi** and forming membrane pores. Toxicities include **arrhythmias, chills and fever, hypotension,** and **nephrotoxicity.**

ID/CC   A 51-year-old chemical engineer who manages the production line at a large petrochemical plant comes to his family doctor for a yearly checkup; he is asymptomatic but is found to have **microscopic hematuria.**

HPI   He is a **heavy smoker** and has been working at the production plant in a variety of capacities over a period of 25 years.

PE   VS: normal. PE: strongly built male with gray hair and smoke discoloration of his mustache and fingertips; a few wheezes heard on lung fields; heart sounds normal; abdominal exam normal; no lymphadenopathy; genitalia normal; rectal exam normal.

Labs   CBC/Lytes: normal. Clinical chemistry and liver function tests normal; blood urea nitrogen (BUN) and creatinine normal. UA: **hematuria; proteinuria.**

Imaging   US: no renoureteral lithiasis; no pelvicalyceal dilatation. Excretory Urography: filling defect and rigidity in wall of urinary bladder.

Gross Pathology   N/A

Micro Pathology   Papanicolaou urine exam shows marked dysplastic and anaplastic transitional cells; cystoscopy and biopsy confirm a **papillary transitional cell carcinoma of the bladder.**

Treatment   Surgery, chemotherapy, radiotherapy.

Discussion   2-amino-1-naphthol and p-diphenylamine are the two carcinogenic substances presumed to be involved in the genesis of transitional cell bladder cancer in individuals exposed to anilines, benzene, and beta-naphthilamines. Saccharin has been shown to induce TCC in rats. Cigarette smoking has a strong association with bladder cancer as well, as does coffee drinking.

ID/CC   A 73-year-old farmer complains of **dry cough** of two months' duration together with intermittent **fever** and increasing **dyspnea.**

HPI   He had a squamous cell carcinoma lesion surgically removed from his nose two months ago and is on **bleomycin** chemotherapy. His is a **smoker.**

PE   Healed skin flap on left nasal fossa; no local lymphadenopathy; multiple freckles and solar dermatitis on scalp; scattered lung **rales and wheezing; soles of feet** show painful, erythematous areas with **skin thickening.**

Labs   CBC/Lytes: normal. Liver function tests do not disclose hepatic damage; blood urea nitrogen (BUN) and creatinine normal.

Imaging   CXR: bilateral pulmonary infiltrates but no evidence of metastatic disease.

Gross Pathology   N/A

Micro Pathology   Interstitial pneumonitis with fibrosis and squamous metaplasia on lung biopsy.

Treatment   Steroids, antibiotics, discontinue bleomycin.

Discussion   Bleomycin is an antibiotic produced by *Streptomyces verticillus* that acts by DNA fragmentation. It is used in a variety of epidermoid and testicular cancers. Fever and chills may ensue with the administration of the drug by any of the parenteral routes available (it is not active orally). It has very little marrow toxicity and almost no immune suppression, but the keratinized areas of the body may suffer from hypertrophy and nail pigmentation. Pulmonary fibrosis is a side effect that characteristically arises in older patients and in those with preexisting lung disease.

ID/CC	A 20-year-old male with testicular cancer presents to his oncologist with a pronounced **decrease in bilateral auditory acuity;** he has also has noticed **edema of his lower legs and eyelids** upon awakening in the morning.
HPI	His last two chemotherapy sessions were administered by an intern who only recently arrived at the municipal hospital.
PE	VS: normal. PE: moderate bilateral **eyelid edema;** auditory testing shows **neurosensory** type of **decreased** bilateral **audition;** lung fields do not show crackles or wheezing; heart sounds rhythmic with no murmurs; abdomen soft with no masses; neurologic exam normal; extremities disclose **pitting edema** in distal third of **lower legs;** foot drop on left side (peripheral neuropathy).
Labs	CBC: normal. Lytes: **hypomagnesemia;** hyperkalemia. **Blood urea nitrogen (BUN) and creatinine increased.**
Imaging	CT - Head: no intracranial causes of hearing loss revealed.
Gross Pathology	N/A
Micro Pathology	N/A
Treatment	Discontinue cisplatin.
Discussion	Cisplatin is an effective chemotherapeutic drug that acts like an alkylating agent, cross-linking via the hydrolysis of chloride groups and reaction with platinum. It is used for bladder and testicular cancers as well as for some ovarian tumors. It can produce severe **renal damage** if administered in the absence of abundant hydration. It also causes CN VIII damage with permanent deafness. Another side effect is peripheral neuropathy, which can be reversed with magnesium.

ID/CC   A 24-year-old female of **Ashkenazi Jewish** background complains to her family doctor of **repeated upper respiratory infections** (due to neutropenia), increasing **fatigue, muscle aches, and headaches.**

HPI   She had been showing flattening of affect, suspiciousness, a delusional mood, and auditory hallucinations that was diagnosed as **schizophrenia** three months ago. She has been receiving **clozapine** treatment ever since.

PE   VS: **fever;** tachycardia (165). PE: patient in obvious discomfort; **pallor** (due to anemia); conscious and oriented to person, place, and time; **petechiae** (due to thrombocytopenia) on chest and arms. ardiopulmonary, abdominal and genital exams normal; no extrapyramidal signs.

Labs   CBC: leukopenia; thrombocytopenia; anemia (= PANCYTOPENIA).

Imaging   CXR: No signs of lung infection.

Gross Pathology   N/A

Micro Pathology   N/A

Treatment   Discontinue clozapine and consider alternate pharmacotherapy.

Discussion   Clozapine is a D4 dopamine receptor blocker used for treatment of schizophrenia and psychosis. Its side effects include mild sedation, anticholinergic, and extrapyramidal symptoms. This patient has drug-induced agranulocytosis, which is characterized by enhanced destruction or myelosuppression. Clozapine causes agranulocytosis in a small percentage of patients (less than 2%). Given the potential lethal effects of this condition, however, patients must receive weekly blood counts. The mechanism is unknown, but an immune reaction may be involved. Agranulocytosis usually reverses with discontinuation of clozapine.

Doxorubicin Cardiotoxicity

ID/CC   A 24-year-old male delivery man for an international courier service currently being treated for **testicular carcinoma,** is brought by ambulance to the ER after **fainting while at work.**

HPI   The patient had noticed a painless lump in his right testicle three months earlier; a biopsy was done and testicular carcinoma was found, for which he was given **doxorubicin** for chemotherapy.

PE   VS: **tachycardia** (110); normotension (BP 118/85). PE: **elevated JVP**; S3 auscultated; **basal rales** in lung fields; **hepatomegaly**; is pitting **edema** in lower legs.

Labs   ECG: ST-T changes, premature venticular contractions; first degree A-V block.

Imaging   CXR: cardiomegaly and pulmonary congestion.

Gross Pathology   Increase in weight and size of heart with softened, weak walls and dilated chambers (= DILATED CARDIOMYOPATHY).

Micro Pathology   N/A

Treatment   Treatment of heart failure due to dilated **cardiomyopathy**. Discontinue doxorubicin.

Discussion   Doxorubicin, also called adriamycin, is an anthracycline antibiotic that binds to DNA and blocks the synthesis of new RNA and/or DNA, thereby blocking cell replication. It is used in treatment of carcinomas of the ovary, breast, testicle, lung, and thyroid. It is also used in the treatment of many types of sarcomas and hematologic cancers. Side effects are mainly cardiac but also may include alopecia and marrow toxicity (myocardiopathy associated with doxorubicin is dose related and irreversible, the mechanisms may be related to the intracellular production of free radicals in myocardium).

Methotrexate Toxicity

ID/CC A 62-year-old female comes to the general oncology unit of the university hospital for **ulceration of the oral mucosa and diarrhea.**

HPI She is being treated for carcinoma of the breast with aggressive methotrexate therapy. Because of impaired renal function, methotrexate toxicity was enhanced. Leucovorin administration did not diminish the cytotoxic effects on normal cells.

PE VS: hypotension (BP 100/50); tachycardia (HR 105). Patient lethargic and dehydrated; oral mucosa and tongue show erythema and shallow ulcers (= BUCCAL STOMATITIS); skin rash on volar aspect of forearms.

Labs CBC: **anemia; thrombocytopenia; leukopenia** (myelosuppression). Blood urea nitrogen (BUN) and creatinine elevated.

Imaging N/A

Gross Pathology N/A

Micro Pathology N/A

Treatment The efficacy of leucovorin therapy depends on early administration when methotrexate toxicity is suspected. Give IV dose equal to or greater than the dose of methotrexate.

Discussion Methotrexate binds reversibly with dihydrofolate reductase, preventing the synthesis of purine and pyrimidine nucleotides. The toxic effects on proliferating tissues are particularly deleterious to the bone marrow, skin, and GI mucosa. Leucovorin "rescue" attenuates some of these toxic effects because it is a metabolically active form of folic acid. For that reason, it does not require reduction by dihydrofolate reductase. Therefore, leucovorin has the capacity to catalyze the one-carbon transfer reactions necessary for purine and pyrimidine biosynthesis.

NSAID-Induced Qualitative Platelet Disorder

ID/CC	A 28-year-old male comes to his family medicine clinic and complains of **increased bruising** over the past three days, as well as **bleeding** from the gums while brushing his teeth.
HPI	The patient is an amateur weight lifter who recently tried to lift an excessive amount of weight but strained a muscle and has been **taking indomethacin** for pain.
PE	VS: normal. PE: athletic male with significant **ecchymoses** on chest and legs bilaterally; blood pressure cuff leaves petechial lines on arms; blood sample site taken on his arrival for routine blood work has become a large ecchymosis.
Labs	CBC/Lytes/UA: normal. Liver function tests normal; **increased prothrombin time (PT)**.
Imaging	N/A
Gross Pathology	N/A
Micro Pathology	N/A
Treatment	Discontinue indomethacin. Vitamin K may be used in patients with an elevated PT.
Discussion	NSAIDs are extensively metabolized and protein-bound. NSAIDs inhibit the enzyme cyclooxygenase, thereby inhibiting prostaglandin production, which in turn produces their antipyretic, anti-inflammatory, and analgesic effects. Aspirin in particular is an irreversible inhibitor, and therefore the production of new platelets (about 8 days) is required before its anticlotting effects can be reversed. Moderate doses of NSAIDs can bring out subclinical platelet defects in otherwise healthy individuals.

ID/CC A 32-year-old male with a prosthetic heart valve complains to his family doctor of **black, tarry stools.**

HPI He had been receiving **oral warfarin** (COUMADIN) to prevent thrombus formation. Two years ago, he had an **aortic valve replacement** due to destruction of the valve secondary to bacterial endocarditis.

PE VS: normotension; pulse rate normal. PE: subconjunctival hemorrhage; bleeding gums; bruises on arms and legs (generalized bleeding).

Labs **Stool guiac positive. UA: hematuria. Markedly elevated prothrombin time** (PT) (affects extrinsic coagulation pathway).

Imaging N/A

Gross Pathology N/A

Micro Pathology N/A

Treatment If significant bleeding and volume depletion have occurred, consider fresh frozen plasma and transfusions. Vitamin K may be required, but careful dosing is necessary for patients with prosthetic heart valves.

Discussion This patient has generalized bleeding, including GI tract bleeding secondary to warfarin treatment. Warfarin compounds inhibit epoxide reductase and hepatic production of the vitamin K-dependent clotting factors (II, VII, IX, and X), interfering with their gamma-carboxylation. Only de novo synthesis is affected; therefore, therapy must continue for 2–3 days before effects are noted. Effects of warfarin last between 5 and 7 days. Warfarin crosses the placenta and is thus contraindicated in pregnant women. Heparin is to be used in this cases.

ID/CC	A 28-year-old female in her 12th week of pregnancy is started on **amantadine prophylaxis,** since the nursing school her 3-year-old daughter attends has had an epidemic of **rubella.**
HPI	One week afterward, she started feeling **dizzy** and having **problems walking normally** (= ATAXIA). An ENT consult ruled out middle-ear causes of vertigo.
PE	VS: **no fever;** remainder of vital signs normal. PE: **speech** somewhat **slurred; gait ataxic;** no focal neurologic signs; normal pregnant breast.
Labs	CBC/Lytes/UA: normal. SMA-12 normal.
Imaging	MR/CT: no intracranial pathology.
Gross Pathology	N/A
Micro Pathology	N/A
Treatment	Discontinue amantadine, avoid contact with daughter for a couple of weeks. Amantadine is not effectively removed by dialysis because of its large volume of distribution.
Discussion	Amantadine is an antiviral agent that blocks viral penetration and uncoating. It also causes the release of dopamine from intact nerve terminals (sometimes used for treatment of Parkinson's disease). It is used as **prophylaxis against influenza A and rubella.** Toxicity includes cerebellar problems such as **ataxic gait, slurred speech,** and **dizziness.** Elderly patients with renal insufficiency are more susceptible to toxicity.

39 Chloramphenicol Side Effects

ID/CC A 31-year-old truck driver visits a health clinic in San Diego complaining of **recurrent infections** (neutropenia), excessive **bleeding** (thrombocytopenia) and malaise, **weakness,** and apathy (anemia).

HPI He travels south of the border daily and eats and sleeps there. He has had **typhoid fever** three times over the past five years, for which he has been treated with high-dose **chloramphenicol.**

PE VS: no fever; normotension. PE: marked **pallor;** oropharynx erythematous with moderate tonsillar exudate; lungs clear; heart sounds normal; generalized **petechiae;** abdominal and neurologic examination unremarkable.

Labs CBC: anemia (Hb 5.7); leukopenia; thrombocytopenia.

Imaging CXR/KUB: within normal limits.

Gross Pathology N/A

Micro Pathology N/A

Treatment Blood transfusions, antithymocyte globulin or cyclosporin, marrow transplantation.

Discussion Chloramphenicol is a bacteriostatic antibiotic that acts by inhibiting peptidyl transferase in the 50S ribosomal unit. It is active against anaerobes (abdominal sepsis) as well as against typhoid fever and meningococcal, streptococcal, and influenzal meningitis. Aplastic anemia is nonetheless a major problem. Some aplastic cases appear to be related to overdose, while others are related to hypersensitivity to the drug. In infants, it produces the **gray-baby syndrome.**

ID/CC   A 37-year-old missionary returning home from central **Africa** comes to the tropical medicine department of the local university for an evaluation of **blurred vision** and seeing **"halos" around lights** at night.

HPI   On directed questioning, he also complains of marked **itching while showering** and notes that his **hair** has been turning prematurely **gray.** He has been taking weekly doses of **chloroquine** for the suppression of hyperendemic malaria.

PE   "Half-moon-shaped" **corneal deposits** on funduscopic exam; diminished visual acuity bilaterally and **retinal edema** with pigmentation; slight **desquamation of palms of hands;** lungs clear; no heart murmurs; no hepatosplenomegaly; no focal neurologic signs.

Labs   CBC: moderate **leukopenia.**

Imaging   CXR: within normal limits.

Gross Pathology   N/A

Micro Pathology   N/A

Treatment   Discontinue chloroquine or change to proguanil as prophylaxis.

Discussion   Chloroquine, a 4-aminoquinoline (acts by blocking DNA and RNA synthesis), is still one of the most widely used drugs for the prophylaxis and treatment of malaria, although resistant strains are becoming increasingly common. Its side effects include headache, dizziness, defects in lens accommodation with frontal heaviness, epigastralgia, diarrhea, and itching (primarily in dark-skinned people). It is also used to treat amebiasis, rheumatoid arthritis, and lupus erythematosus. When taken for long periods, it produces retinal edema with macular hyperpigmentation and chloroquine deposits with visual field defects as well as semicircular corneal opacities.

ID/CC	A 12-year-old girl is brought to the pediatric emergency room by her parents because of the development of **double vision** (= DIPLOPIA), blurred vision, and **difficulty swallowing** (= DYSPHAGIA).
HPI	Three days ago she had gone to her grandmother's house in the country, where she ate plum jam (canned, homemade food).
PE	Patient **hypothermic** and dyspneic but is well oriented and conscious with **generalized muscle weakness;** diplopia and bilateral eyelid drooping (= PTOSIS); **pupils mydriatic and do not respond to light or accommodation;** no alterations in sensibility; mouth dry and voice hoarse; abdomen slightly distended; peristaltic sounds scarce.
Labs	Plum jam was analyzed and tested postive for botulinum toxin.
Imaging	CXR: normal. CT - Head: normal.
Gross Pathology	N/A
Micro Pathology	N/A
Treatment	Horse-pooled trivalent (A, B and E) antitoxin. ICU care with ventilatory support.
Discussion	Botulinum toxin is produced by *Clostridium botulinum*, a spore-forming anaerobe. The powerful toxin is a preformed, heat-labile zinc metalloprotease that characteristically **inhibits the release of acetylcholine** at the synaptic clefts of cholinergic nerve terminals. Canned foods are the reservoir most of the time, and intoxication produces generalized muscle weakness with a flaccid paralysis and possible death due to respiratory paralysis.

ID/CC A 21-year-old college baseball player restarted his training three days ago running 1600 meters a day in preparation for the upcoming state tournament; yesterday he hit a home run and started off to first base when he suddenly fell to the ground and **could not walk** due to **acute pain** in the **Achilles tendon**.

HPI He had spent four weeks in the hospital recovering from perforated appendicitis with peritonitis, where he received **IV ciprofloxacin** for two weeks due to surgical wound infection with *Pseudomonas aeruginosa* that was resistant to all other antibiotics.

PE Surgical wound completely healed with no evidence of infection or postincisional hernia; Penrose drain orifice within normal limits; **inability to dorsiflex left foot; Achilles tendon completely severed.**

Labs CBC: no leukocytosis; no anemia. SMA-7 normal. UA: normal.

Imaging CXR/KUB: within normal limits

Gross Pathology N/A

Micro Pathology Achilles tendon shows inflammatory neutrophilic infiltrate with areas of hemorrhage and necrosis.

Treatment Surgical repair.

Discussion Fluoroquinolones such as ciprofloxacin and norfloxacin are bactericidal antibiotics active against gram-negative rods, including *Pseudomonas*; they are also active against *Neisseria* and some gram-positive organisms. They act by inhibiting DNA gyrase (= TOPOISOMERASE II). Side effects include damage to cartilage (contraindicated in pregnancy and small children), tendonitis, and tendon rupture; they also produce gastric upset and nausea and may cause superinfections.

ID/CC   A 23-year-old marathon runner visits his sports-medicine doctor complaining of unsightly, embarrassing **growth of his right breast** (= GYNECOMASTIA) as well as **undue fatigue** after training and a slight yellowish hue in his eyes (= JAUNDICE).

HPI   Three months ago, he was put on daily oral **ketoconazole** because he had been suffering from a refractory fungal infection of his toenails (= ONYCHOMYCOSIS).

PE   VS: bradycardia; hypotension (BP 100/60) (athlete's heart); **fever** (38.1 C). PE: slight jaundice in conjunctiva; no lymphadenopathy; pupils equal and reactive to light and accommodation; no neck masses; cardiopulmonary exam normal; no hepatomegaly on abdominal exam; remainder of PE unremarkable.

Labs   **AST and ALT increased;** serum bilirubin level increased.

Imaging   US - Liver: mildly enlarged liver.

Gross Pathology   N/A

Micro Pathology   N/A

Treatment   Discontinue drug, local treatment of mycosis, temporary nail removal if necessary.

Discussion   Ketoconazole is an imidazole that inhibits fungal synthesis of ergosterol in membranes. It is used for blastomycosis, coccidioidomycosis, histoplasmosis, and candidiasis. Major side effects are hepatic damage, gynecomastia, impotence (due to inhibition of testosterone synthesis), inhibition of cytochrome P450, fever, and chills. When taken with antacids or H_2 receptor blockers, its absorption is decreased. It dramatically increases cyclosporine levels.

ID/CC	A 21-year-old comes to the health clinic because of the development of **fever,** marked **itching** all over his body, a **generalized rash** with joint swelling, and **difficulty breathing.**
HPI	He just returned from a atrip abroad, where he had developed a **purulent urethral discharge** (gonococcal urethritis) and went to a local doctor, who gave him "two shots on each side" preceded by two pills (procaine penicillin and probenecid).
PE	VS: mild **hypotension.** PE: patient in acute distress; mild cyanosis, and difficulty breathing; **generalized lymphadenopathy** and large **hives** on hands and chest.
Labs	CBC: leukocytosis (12,000 with 60% neutrophils). UA: **proteinuria.** Lytes: normal.
Imaging	CXR: normal.
Gross Pathology	N/A
Micro Pathology	N/A
Treatment	Subcutaneous epinephrine, oxygen, hydrocortisone, antihistamines. Maintain airway and provide assisted ventilation if necessary. Severe reactions may result in laryngeal obstruction, hypotension, and death.
Discussion	Penicillins are antimicrobial drugs that block cell wall synthesis by inhibiting peptidoglycan cross-linking; they are bactericidal for gram-positive cocci and rods, gram-negative cocci, and spirochetes such as *Treponema pallidum*. Most adverse reactions to penicillins are allergic reactions. Sensitization occurs in proportion to the dose and duration of past exposure. Anaphylactic (= TYPE 1 HYPERSENSITIVITY) reaction involves antigen reacting with IgE on presensitized mast cells and basophils; it is usually severe and immediate. Penicillin may also give rise to a serum sickness (= TYPE 3 HYPERSENSITIVITY) reaction, an immune complex disorder with a lag period during which antibodies are formed, as in this case.

ID/CC   A 19-year-old military recruit comes to his medical officer complaining of **red urine** and **orange-colored staining of his T-shirt;** he also complains that every time he takes rifampin, he feels as if he has the flu (flu-like response).

HPI   He underwent a routine physical exam and laboratory tests prior to joining the military camp and was started on **rifampin** at that time (meningococcus was found on nasopharyngeal secretions, indicating a meningococcal carrier state).

PE   VS: normal. PE: muscular male in no acute distress; no jaundice, hepatomegaly, spider angiomas, or parotid enlargement; nonpruritic maculopapular **rash** on chest and **petechial hemorrhages** on limbs.

Labs   AST and AST moderately **increased.** UA: **proteinuria** (light chain). CBC: **thrombocytopenia.**

Imaging   CXR/KUB: normal.

Gross Pathology   N/A

Micro Pathology   N/A

Treatment   Switch to penicillin or ceftriaxone.

Discussion   Rifampin is an antituberculous drug that acts by inhibiting DNA-dependent RNA polymerase. It also acts against meningococci. One of its major drawbacks is the rapid development of resistance if used alone. Untoward side effects include discoloration of urine and sweat with a yellowish-orange hue, hepatic damage, skin rash, thrombocytopenia, tubulointerstitial nephritis, and increased metabolism of anticoagulants and HIV protease inhibitors.

ID/CC An asymptomatic **HIV-positive** 29-year-old male visited his infectious-disease specialist for a routine checkup; after finding his **CD4 (410)**, the physician decided to start him on oral **zidovudine** (= AZT) at a dosage of 600 mg/day.

HPI Two months later, he returns to the doctor's office feeling very **tired** (due to anemia); he has also had two upper respiratory infections and yesterday started **bleeding** from his gums (due to thrombocytopenia).

PE VS: slight tachycardia. PE: marked **pallor**; **disseminated petechiae** in arms and legs.

Labs CBC: **decreased platelets** (= THROMBOCYTOPENIA); **decreased WBCs** (= NEUTROPENIA); **decreased RBCs** (= ANEMIA).

Imaging N/A

Gross Pathology N/A

Micro Pathology N/A

Treatment Discontinue AZT and **switch to zalcitabine.**

Discussion A nucleoside analog used as an antiretroviral agent in symptomatic patients or in those with CD4 counts < 500. It is often combined with dideoxyinosine (ddI) and acts by inhibiting HIV reverse transcriptase. Toxicity includes **thrombocytopenia, anemia, and neutropenia.**

ID/CC   A 24-year-old female visits her physician because of **pain in her arm** after spending all day cleaning the basement of her house; x-rays taken as a routine procedure revealed a **linear fracture** of the right radius.

HPI   She is an epileptic who has been treated for three years with **phenytoin.** She states that she has been suffering from increasing **leg weakness** and persistent **lower back pain.**

PE   VS: normal. PE: **increase in size of gums** (= GINGIVAL HYPERPLASIA); no neck masses; no lymphadenopathy; chest normal to auscultation; abdomen soft with no masses; no neurologic signs; **hirsutism** present; linear right radial fracture; **tenderness of lumbar vertebrae** and pelvic rim **on palpation.**

Labs   Hb 10 g/dL; blood urea nitrogen (BUN) and creatinine normal. Lytes: normal. **Increased alkaline phosphatase; decreased levels of vitamin D; hypocalcemia; hypophosphatemia.**

Imaging   XR: right radial fracture; **shortening of lumbar vertebrae; generalized osteopenia and Looser's lines** (= MILKMAN'S FRACTURES; PATHOGNOMONIC).

Gross Pathology   N/A

Micro Pathology   N/A

Treatment   Switch to other antiepileptics, vitamin D, calcium supplements; treat fracture, physiotherapy.

Discussion   Phenytoin and, to a lesser extent, other antiepileptic drugs such as phenobarbital and carbamazepine may cause target organ resistance to vitamin D with consequent development of osteomalacia (in adults) and rickets (in children). Fractures with minor trauma may be a presenting sign, as may bone pain and proximal muscle weakness.

Barbiturate Intoxication

ID/CC A 19-year-old **epileptic** student is brought by ambulance to the emergency room in a **coma** after being found on the floor of her apartment.

HPI She had been feeling **depressed** for several months and, according to her roommate, had just broken up with her boyfriend and took a **whole bottle of her antiepileptic pills** at once (phenobarbital).

PE She was brought to the ER **unconscious, hypotensive, hypothermic** (35 C), and **bradypneic**. PE: no response to verbal stimulation; reacts only to painful stimuli; **bullae** on lower legs; deep tendon reflexes slow (= HYPOREFLEXIA).

Labs ABGs: pronounced **hypoxemia** and **respiratory acidosis**. Blood alcohol level also increased. ECG: sinus bradycardia.

Imaging CXR: no evidence of aspiration (a common complication of sedative overdose due to diminished gag reflex and altered consciousness).

Gross Pathology Globus pallidus necrosis with pulmonary and cerebral edema.

Micro Pathology N/A

Treatment Airway maintenance; oxygen; assisted ventilation; gastric lavage; cathartics; alkalinization of urine; warming blankets; consider pressors or dialysis. **Flumazenil reverses benzodiazepine overdose but not barbiturate overdose.**

Discussion Barbiturates facilitate GABA action by increasing the duration of the chloride channel opening; they are used as antianxiety drugs, in sleep disorders, and in anesthesia. Barbiturates **induce the cytochrome P450 system** of liver microsomal enzymes, thereby affecting the metabolism of several drugs. In overdose, death may ensue due to severe **respiratory depression** or **aspiration pneumonia**.

ID/CC A 45-year-old **female** comes to her family physician for an evaluation of frequent upper respiratory infections (due to neutropenia) and gum bleeding (due to thrombocytopenia). She also complains of **double vision** (= DIPLOPIA), nausea, **sleepiness,** and **dry mouth** as well as difficulty walking.

HPI She has been suffering from recurrent, **severe, sharp pain on the left side of her face** that radiates to the corner of her eye and is triggered by mastication or cold exposure (= TRIGEMINAL NEURALGIA). She has been taking **carbamazepine** for several months, during which time her attacks have been much less frequent.

PE VS: normal. PE: patient well hydrated, oriented, and in no acute distress; **ataxic gait;** funduscopic exam normal aside from mild **mydriasis** (anticholinergic effect).

Labs CBC: **decreased platelets; decreased neutrophil count.** Coagulation and bleeding time increased. LP: CSF normal. No evidence of multiple sclerosis on evoked-potential testing; **AST and ALT** moderately **increased.**

Imaging CT - Brain: normal.

Gross Pathology N/A

Micro Pathology N/A

Treatment Switch to phenytoin. If failure of medical treatment, posterior fossa surgical exploration is warranted in selected cases.

Discussion Trigeminal neuralgia is sometimes seen in association with multiple sclerosis, primarily in younger patients. Carbamazepine is chemically very similar to imipramine and has been used for trigeminal neuralgia as well as for the treatment of convulsions. Side effects include blurred vision, dry mouth, inability to start urination, lightheadedness, aplastic anemia, hepatotoxicity, diplopia, ataxic gait, and nausea.

ID/CC A neonatologist is called upon to evaluate a newborn with multiple birth defects.

HPI The mother is a 17-year-old runaway who is homeless, had no prenatal care, and continued her habit of **getting drunk** two or three times a week throughout her pregnancy.

PE **Low birth weight; small head size** (= MICROCEPHALY); **facial flattening** with **epicanthal folds;** small eyes (= MICROPHTHALMOS); **cardiac murmur** (diagnosed as an atrial septal defect); hirsutism; positive Ortolani's sign on left hip and lack of complete hip abduction on that side; chest deformed (pectus excavatum).

Labs CBC: mild anemia. Increased AST and ALT.

Imaging CXR: cardiomegaly; pectus excavatum deformity. XR - Hip: congenital dislocation of left hip.

Gross Pathology N/A

Micro Pathology N/A

Treatment No specific treatment available; treat each malformation/disease accordingly

Discussion Alcohol is the leading cause of fetal malformations in the U.S. Fetal alcohol syndrome may cause myriad abnormalities, both skeletal and visceral, but usually involves a triad of features: (1) craniofacial dysmorphology, including mild to moderate **microcephaly** and **maxillary hypoplasia;** (2) prenatal and postnatal **growth retardation;** and (3) CNS abnormalities, including **mental retardation,** with IQs often in the range of 50–70. In addition, fetal alcohol exposure leads to an increased incidence of **cardiac malformations,** including **patent ductus arteriosus** and **septal defects.** Risk is dose related.

ID/CC A 23-year-old female is suing her physician for sexually abusing her while he was **reducing her left dislocated shoulder.**

HPI She injured her shoulder while rock climbing in Colorado. The doctor was called upon to see her immediately after the accident. She did not suffer major injuries but had a dislocated shoulder and was not cooperative enough to tolerate the procedure (reduction) without medication, so he anesthetized her with **ketamine**, atropine, and diazepam.

PE

Labs N/A

Imaging X-rays at time of injury showed an anterior shoulder dislocation.

Gross Pathology N/A

Micro Pathology N/A

Treatment The addition of diazepam and atropine often diminishes the hallucinogenic effect of ketamine.

Discussion Ketamine is an arylcyclohexylamine that produces a dissociative anesthesia; the patient has open eyes and her muscle tone is preserved (with sufficient analgesia to do major surgery and total amnesia). Its major side effect is vivid hallucinations, sometimes terrifying, upon arousal, mostly in adults. It is widely used in developing countries as well as in rural areas where there is no available anesthesiologist, and in short pediatric procedures (abscess debridement, burn wounds dressing changes, etc.) because of its relative safety and lack of life-threatening side effects (such as respiratory depression, which is common with other anesthetics).

ID/CC   An 82-year-old male complains to his doctor about chronic **nausea** and vomiting as well as **involuntary tremors, chewing, and grimacing movements** (= DYSKINESIA).

HPI   The patient also states he has been having **palpitations** and **insomnia**. He suffers from Parkinson's disease and has been taking **levodopa** for a long time.

PE   VS: **tachycardia** (115); **postural hypotension.** PE: patient thin; typical Parkinsonian gait; masklike facies; pill-rolling tremor of hands; choreiform movements of head and hands; grimacing facial movements.

Labs   CBC/PBS: **Coombs' test positive**; no hemolytic anemia. Growth hormone level increased. ECG: **ventricular premature contractions** (cause of palpitations).

Imaging   N/A

Gross Pathology   N/A

Micro Pathology   N/A

Treatment   Minimize side effects by taking drug with meals or in smaller doses or by taking antacids; tolerance to emetic effect may also develop. Antiemetics may be given, but these may reduce antiparkinsonian effects.

Discussion   Dopamine cannot cross blood-brain barrier; however, levodopa, a precursor of dopamine, does. When this drug is given, it is usually in combination with carbidopa, an inhibitor of the peripheral dopa decarboxylase (thus increasing the half-life and plasma levels of levodopa). Dyskinesias are a common side effect, as are GI symptoms (NAUSEA AND VOMITING) and postural hypotension. Arrhythmias, anxiety, depression, insomnia, and confusion have also been reported. Levodopa dose must be slowly decreased, since **abrupt cessation** may result in an **akinetic state.**

ID/CC	A 32-year-old male is brought by his wife to the family care center of the community because of increasing **tremors, slowing of movements** (= BRADYKINESIA), and **postural instability.**
HPI	The patient works as a **chemist** at a leading pharmaceutical research company in Northern California and has a long-standing history of **drug abuse requiring hospitalization.**
PE	VS: normal. PE: flat facies; **resting tremor; cogwheel rigidity;** impaired capacity for voluntary motor activity; speech slow, as are voluntary movements.
Labs	N/A
Imaging	CT - Head: no apparent intracranial pathology.
Gross Pathology	N/A
Micro Pathology	N/A
Treatment	No effective therapies currently exist for treatment of drug-induced Parkinson's syndrome aside from discontinuation of offending drug.
Discussion	Several drugs may produce Parkinson-like symptoms, including haloperidol and phenothiazines, which block dopamine receptors, as well as reserpine and tetrabenazine, which deplete biogenic monoamines from their storage sites. In their attempts to produce "designer drugs" related to meperidine, "underground" chemists have also synthesized a compound, 1-methyl-4-phenyl-tetrahydrobiopteridine (MPTP). The toxicity of MPTP is produced by its oxidation to **MPP +** (a toxic compound), which selectively **destroys the dopaminergic neurons** in the **substantia nigra.**

ID/CC   A 21-year-old male who emigrated to the U.S. three months ago visits a neighborhood medical clinic complaining of apprehension, tremors, **dizziness, inability to walk properly, and double vision.**

HPI   He is a newly diagnosed epileptic whose understanding of English is very poor, so when his doctor prescribed one tablet of **phenytoin** *every 24 hours*, he thought the doctor meant one tablet *every two to four hours.*

PE   Intention **tremors** and **ataxic gait; nystagmus** present, but funduscopic exam normal; generalized **lymphadenopathy;** chest auscultated normally; **hepatomegaly** with no peritoneal signs on abdominal exam; skin **rash** on dorsum of hands and chest.

Labs   CBC: megaloblastic anemia; neutrophils highly lobular and segmented. Moderate increases in AST and ALT.

Imaging   CXR: within normal limits for age. CT - Head: no intracranial pathology in evidence.

Gross Pathology   N/A

Micro Pathology   N/A

Treatment   Gastric lavage if acute overdose. Stop treatment temporarily, then resume at proper dosage.

Discussion   Phenytoin is used for the prevention of grand mal and psychomotor seizures. Phenytoin alters ionic conductances (sodium), membrane potentials, and concentrations of certain neurotransmitters. Chronic use also induces microsomal enzymes. Other side effects include skin rashes, lymphadenopathy, and megaloblastic anemia (causes impaired DNA synthesis and folic acid deficiencies by interfering with folic acid absorption by inhibiting folate conjugases). **Diplopia** and **ataxia** are common dose-related side effects; **gingival hyperplasia** and **hirsutism** are known to occur as well. Chronic use may also cause abnormalities in **vitamin D metabolism,** which results in **osteomalacia.**

ID/CC A 20-year-old medical student is brought to the emergency room because his roommate noticed that he had been **sleeping all day** and awakening from time to time with **nightmares;** the patient then stated that **he wanted to shoot himself** and began to look for a gun.

HPI He had just finished end-of-year exams in all his subjects, for which he had studied late into the night and had taken **methylphenidate** daily for several weeks.

PE VS: mild tachycardia. PE: when asked questions, patient is well oriented with respect to time, person, and place but is very **lethargic** and complains of a severe **headache;** funduscopic exam normal; no increased JVP; no neck masses; lungs clear; heart sounds with no murmurs; abdomen soft and nontender with no masses; peristaltic sounds increased (patient complains of abdominal cramps when these are heard).

Labs Routine lab exams fail to disclose abnormality; urine tox screen shows only trace amounts of amphetamine.

Imaging CXR: no cardiopulmonary pathology apparent.

Gross Pathology N/A

Micro Pathology N/A

Treatment Hospitalization due to risk of suicide, antidepressants, supportive treatment.

Discussion Amphetamines are used recreationally for their ability to produce a sense of well-being and euphoria, with sympathetic stimulation. There are also some medical indications for their use, such as hyperactive child syndrome. Amphetamines may be abused orally as well as parenterally, or they may be smoked. Withdrawal symptoms include lethargy, suicidal thoughts, profound depression, intestinal colic, headache, sleepiness, and nightmares.

ID/CC A 26-year-old female who models for photography magazines is referred to the dermatologist by her family doctor because of of **persistent acne** that has beenunresponsive to the usual treatment.

HPI She also complains of **constant thirst** and **urination** as well as dryness of the mouth. She has been diagnosed with **bipolar affective disorder** with **manic** predominance and was recently started on **lithium therapy.**

PE Sensorium normal; oriented and cooperative; **mouth is dry**; no signs of present depression or mania; face shows presence of **severe cystic acne** in vicinity of chin, forehead, and upper chest with **folliculitis.**

Labs CBC: **leukocytosis.** Pregnancy test negative. ECG: T-wave inversion.

Imaging N/A

Gross Pathology N/A

Micro Pathology N/A

Treatment Acne treatment with isotretinoin (teratogenic), chronic, low-dose tetracycline, benzoyl peroxide.

Discussion Lithium is the preferred treatment for the manic stage of bipolar affective disorder; however, its mechanism of action on mood stability is still unclear. One possibility revolves around lithium's effects on the IP_3 second-messenger system in the brain. Lithium inhibits the degradation of IP_2 to IP_1 and IP_1 to inositol. The net effect is to increase IP_3 levels and promote its cellular effects. The onset of action make take several days, and side effects may be very bothersome, such as persistent polyuria and polydipsia (ADH antagonism), weight gain, and severe acne. It is contraindicated in pregnancy due to its teratogenic effect.

ID/CC A 27-year-old female is brought to the emergency room by her mother because of a **high fever** and **muscle rigidity.**

HPI The patient's mother reports that her daughter is being treated with **antipsychotics** for schizophrenia but is otherwise in good health.

PE VS: **tachycardia** (165); **hypotension** (BP 100/50), **fever.** PE: patient **confused** with an altered level of consciousness; pallor; **diaphoresis** (due to autonomic instability); marked rigidity of all muscle groups.

Labs CBC: **leukocytosis. Increased creatine kinase (CK)** (indicates muscle damage). ABG: metabolic **acidosis.**

Imaging N/A

Gross Pathology N/A

Micro Pathology N/A

Treatment Treat muscle rigidity with diazepam and **initiate rapid cooling** to prevent brain damage (fever may reach dangerous levels). Dantrolene, dopamine agonists (= BROMOCRIPTINE). Respiratory support.

Discussion Neuroleptic malignant syndrome is a life-threatening complication characterized by generalized rigidity and high fever that occurs in certain patients with idiosyncracy to antypsychotics, mainly haloperidol. The onset of symptoms usually is within a couple of weeks after the drug is started, diminished iron reserves and dehydration are predisposing factors.

ID/CC A 26-year-old female is brought to the ER by her boss after **fainting** at work. The day before she complained of a **dry mouth** along with **constipation and urinary retention.**

HPI She had a major manic episode of hyperactivity and productivity at work two months ago, as well as auditory hallucinations, for which she was diagnosed with a schizoaffective disorder and has been undergoing treatment with the antipsychotic drug **thioridazine.**

PE VS: **orthostatic hypotension; tachycardia** (108/min). PE: acute **depression; dryness of mouth;** inability to accomodate normally (= with resultant blurred vision); funduscopic exam shows **pigmentary retinopathy; dilated pupils;** abdomen slightly distended with diminished peristaltic movements.

Labs Increased prolactin levels, hyperglycemia, ECG: flattened T wave, appearance of U waves, Q-T segment prolongation.

Imaging N/A

Gross Pathology N/A

Micro Pathology N/A

Treatment Discontinue offending drug.

Discussion Antipsychotic drugs such as thioridazine, chlorpromazine, and haloperidol manifest a number of adverse effects, making drug compliance difficult. Muscarinic blockade produces typical anticholinergic effects such as tachycardia, loss of accommodation, urinary retention, and constipation. Alpha blockade produces **orthostatic hypotension.** Other side effect include **extrapyramidal signs** (= AKATHISIA, TARDIVE DYSKINESIA, AKINESIA, DYSTYONIA, CONVULSIONS). Pigmentary retinopathy is restricted to thioridazine use.

ID/CC	A 52-year-old college professor with a history of **schizophrenia** presents with **tremor and rigidity**.
HPI	The patient is **diabetic** and a **smoker** and has been receiving **antipsychotic** therapy for **many years**.
PE	**Abnormal facial gestures,** including **lip smacking, jaw muscle spasms,** and jerky movements around mouth; Increased blinking frequency and difficulty with speech.
Labs	All labs normal.
Imaging	XR - Skull: **calcification of pineal gland.**
Gross Pathology	N/A
Micro Pathology	N/A
Treatment	Decreasing dose or discontinuing antipsychotic drugs is first step. Benzodiazepines treatment can often improve GABAergic activity and therefore alleviate symptoms. Propranolol and calcium channel blockers may be of use.
Discussion	Tardive dyskinesia is a syndrome characterized by late-occurring abnormal **choreoathetoid movements.** It is often associated with antipsychotic drugs (e.g., dopamine blockers) and is estimated to affect about 30% of patients receiving treatment (males and females affected equally). Predisposing factors include older age, smoking and diabetes. Advanced cases of tardive dyskinesia may be irreversible, so **early recognition of symptoms is critical.**

Tricyclic Antidepressant Overdose

ID/CC A 5-year-old male is rushed to the emergency department after his mother found him playing with her purse, where she carries her **antidepressants** (imipramine); she noticed that the boy swallowed a handful of pills

HPI The child complained of **dry mouth, blurred vision, and hot cheeks** (anticholinergic effect); he also complained of **palpitations** (due to arrhythmias).

PE VS: tachycardia with irregular rhythm; **fever** (anticholinergic inability to sweat); hypotension. PE: patient **confused**; pupils dilated (= MYDRIASIS); **skin warm and red; diminished peristalsis** with no peritoneal signs.

Labs Lytes: normal. Blood urea nitrogen (BUN) and creatine phosphokinase (CPK) normal. UA: **myoglobin** present. ECG: occasional PVCs (= PREMATURE VENTRICULAR CONTRACTIONS) and **prolonged QRS and PR intervals.**

Imaging CXR: no pathology found.

Gross Pathology N/A

Micro Pathology N/A

Treatment Gastric lavage, activated charcoal, physostigmine in selected cases. Dialysis is not effective for TCA overdose because TCAs have a wide volume of distribution

Discussion Tricyclic antidepressants (imipramine, amitriptyline, doxepin) block the reuptake of norepinephrine and serotonin and are used for endogenous depression treatment. TCAs are commonly taken by suicidal patients and are a major cause of poisoning and death. Intoxication or overdose may produce. **seizures** and **myoclonic jerking** (most common clinical presentation) with **rhabdomyolysis. Death may occur within a few hours.** Other side effects are anticholinergic (**sedation, coma, xerostomia, and diminished bowel sounds**).

ID/CC   A 5-year-old child becomes **cyanotic** and has a cardiorespiratory **arrest** in the ER.

HPI   The child, a known asthmatic, had come to the by ambulance 15 minutes earlier with severe **wheezing, intercostal retractions, nasal flaring, and marked dyspnea.** He was given inhaled corticosteroids.

PE   Immediate CPR was given, the patient was intubated and assisted ventilation administered. The patient came out of the arrest but then returned to his pre-admission state of wheezing and respiratory failure.

Labs   CBC: **leukocytosis** (16,000) with neutrophilia. ABGs: mixed respiratory and metabolic acidosis with hypoxemia and hypercapnia. **Peak expiratory flow rate (PEFR) markedly reduced** (indicates severe airway obstruction).

Imaging   CXR: left lower lobe infiltrate compatible with pneumonia.

Gross Pathology   N/A

Micro Pathology   N/A

Treatment   Metaproterenol by inhalation until bronchospasms stop. Treat infection, acid-base-electrolyte imbalance.

Discussion   In a severe case of asthma like this, a preexisting infection is usually the precipitating event. Inhaled steroids have no place in the treatment of an acute attack such as this, as is also the case with sodium cromolyn (cromolyn prevents the release of mast cell mediators, useful for prophylaxis). IV steroids may be given but may take several hours to take full effect (they block leukotriene synthesis by blocking phospholipase A2). Inhaled beta agonists are the mainstay of acute, emergent therapy (they activate adenyl cyclase and thereby increase cAMP, which relaxes bronchial smooth muscle). Adverse effects include arrhythmias, tachycardia, and tremors.

ID/CC   A 45-year-old female who works as a preschool teacher complains of **fatigue,** headache, dizziness, **shortness of breath,** and **constipation.**

HPI   She has been receiving **amiodarone** for one year for treatment for chronic palpitations that arose spontaneously, with tachycardia that reaches 220 beats per minute and increases when she drinks coffee, was under stress tor smoke (= SUPRAVENTRICULAR TACHYCARDIA).

PE   VS: **bradycardia** (55); normotension; no fever. PE: well-hydrated, conscious, oriented; neck no masses or bruit in neck; **diffuse crackling sounds and wheezes** in both lung fields, predominantly in bases; abdominal and neurologic exams normal.

Labs   ECG: **prolonged QT interval** and QRS duration. **AST and ALT moderately elevated.**

Imaging   CXR: bilateral intestitial infiltrates bilaterally (incipient pulmonary fibrosis).

Gross Pathology   N/A

Micro Pathology   N/A

Treatment   Continuously monitor ECG and vital signs. Sodium bicarbonate may reverse cardiac depressant effects if evident. Discontinue drug if evidence of pulmonary fibrosis.

Discussion   Amiodarone is a Class IA antiarrhythmic drug that acts by blocking the sodium channel. Adverse reactions require careful monitoring and include **thyroid dysfunction** (both hypo- and hyperthyroidism), **constipation, hepatocellular necrosis,** and **pulmonary fibrosis,** which may be fatal. It may also produce **bradycardia** and **heart block** in susceptible individuals. Amiodarone has a **long half-life,** so if toxicity occurs, it persists long after the drug has been discontinued.

ID/CC	A 30-year-old man is brought to the emergency room in a **stuporous state** with nausea, **protracted vomiting**, and malaise.
HPI	He had been overtreating himself with Tylenol (acetaminophen) with up to 30 pills a day to relieve the pain and discomfort associated with a whiplash neck injury he sustained approximately a week ago.
PE	VS: normal. PE: **icterus; asterixis;** patient slightly **confused** and **dehydrated;** funduscopic exam normal; physical exam otherwise normal.
Labs	Markedly **elevated serum transaminases; elevated serum bilirubin; prolonged prothrombin time (PT);** mildly elevated serum creatinine and blood urea nitrogen (BUN); mild hypoglycemia. ABGs: **metabolic acidosis. Serum acetaminophen levels in toxic range.**
Imaging	CXR: Within normal limits.
Gross Pathology	N/A
Micro Pathology	Overt coagulative centrilobular necrosis on liver biopsy; cells appear shrunken and pyknotic with marked presence of neutrophils.
Treatment	**N-acetylcysteine as a specific antidote** to replete hepatic glutathione levels; supportive management of fulminant hepatic and renal failure; consider liver transplant in severe cases.
Discussion	One of the products of cytochrome P-450 metabolism of acetaminophen is hepatotoxic. This reactive metabolite is normally detoxified by glutathione in the liver, but in large doses it may overwhelm the liver's capacity for detoxification. Renal damage may occur because of metabolism by the kidney. Encephalopathy, coma, and death may occur without treatment.

ID/CC   A 47-year-old obese male who has been a heavy smoker for 20 years (with COPD) visits his family doctor complaining of malaise, lack of appetite (= ANOREXIA), and persistent **pain in his shoulders and lower back** together with **dyspnea and dizziness.**

HPI   He recently had a recurrence of gastroesophageal reflux disease, and nothing but his **aluminum gel** relieves it, so he has been taking large quantities of it in order to relieve his symptoms.

PE   Patient obese and **lethargic;** heart sounds with no murmurs; lungs have a few scattered rales in both bases; **petechial hemorrhages** in legs and arms.

Labs   CBC: mild hemolytic **anemia** (increased erythrocyte fragility); platelet count normal (but there are abnormalities in function-adhesion). **Phosphorus serum level low;** increased LDH.

Imaging   XR: no sign of osteomalacia (acute phosphorus deficiency, not chronic).

Gross Pathology   N/A

Micro Pathology   N/A

Treatment   Phosphorus supplements and/or switch to other antacids or H_2 receptor blockers.

Discussion   Aluminum salts (HYDROXIDE) are used as antacids in many preparations. They commonly produce **constipation,** which is why most compounds add magnesium for its laxative properties to counteract the effects of aluminum. Another side effect of aluminum therapy is impaired absorption of phosphorus in the GI tract. With diminished available phosphate, the concentration of 2,3- diphosphoglycerate (2,3-DPG) decreases, leading to abnormal tissue oxygenation (malaise, dyspnea) and muscle weakness (including respiratory muscles). Hypophosphatemia, if persistent, may lead to osteomalacia.

ID/CC   A 48-year-old factory worker is brought to the ER after a **chemical spill** because of **difficulty breathing** and **irritation** of the **eyes** and **throat.**

HPI   He denies allergies, previous surgical operations, diabetes, high blood pressure, infectious diseases, trauma, blood transfusions, hospitalizations and he is not on any current medication.

PE   VS: normal. PE: patient conscious, alert, oriented, in no acute distress; **ammonia smell** emanating from clothes; **marked hyperemia** of ocular conjunctiva and upper respiratory passageways; throat mucosa and tongue **edematous** with mucosal **sloughing** on the left side; no laryngospasm; lungs clear to auscultation; abdomen is soft with no masses or peritoneal signs; no focal neurologic signs.

Labs   CBC/Lytes: normal. US: normal.

Imaging   CXR: no evidence of pneumomediastinum (seen with esophageal perforation with ammonia ingestion).

Gross Pathology   N/A

Micro Pathology   N/A

Treatment   Treatment depends on route of exposure to ammonia gas. Observe patient for upper airway obstruction due to inhalation injuries. For eyes and skin, wash exposed regions with water or saline. There are no specific antidotes for this or other caustic burns.

Discussion   Ammonia is used as a fertilizer, household chemical, and commercial cleaning agent. Ammonia gas is highly water soluble and produces its **corrosive effects** on contact with tissues such as the eyes and respiratory tract, producing severe laryngitis and tracheitis with possible laryngospasm.

ID/CC   An 18-year-old high-school dropout is brought to the ER because of marked **restlessness, euphoria, anxiety, tachycardia, paranoia,** and **agitation.**

HPI   The patient is a known **drug abuser** with an otherwise-unremarkable medical history.

PE   VS: marked **hypertension** (BP 185/100); **tachycardia** (165). PE: **diaphoresis; tremor.**

Labs   Amphetamine levels are detectable in **urine** and gastric samples. UA: **occult hemoglobin** (due to **rhabdomyolysis** with **myoglobinuria**).

Imaging   N/A

Gross Pathology   N/A

Micro Pathology   N/A

Treatment   Treat agitation, seizures, and coma if they occur. Hypertension best treated with vasodilator such as nitroprusside. Propranolol used to prevent tachyarrhythmias.

Discussion   A variety of amphetamines are used clinically, including methylphenidate (Ritalin) for attention deficit hyperactivity disorder (ADHD). However, many of these drugs are commonly abused as well. Such agents activate CNS via peripheral release of catecholamines, inhibition of reuptake mechanisms, or inhibition of monoamine oxidase enzymes. Excretion is dependent on urine pH, with optimal excretion occurring in acidified urine.

ID/CC A 10-year-old boy living near a pigment-manufacturing industry presents with a **burning sensation** in a **glove-and-stocking distribution** together with severe **bilateral arm and leg weakness**.

HPI He also presents with **hyperpigmentation** and thickening of the skin over his palms and soles. The child is in the habit of **eating paint**.

PE Hyperkeratosis on palms and soles; peculiar **"raindrop" depigmentation; Aldrich–Mees lines** over nails; neurologic exam reveals decreased sensation, decreased motor strength, absent deep tendon reflexes, and wasting (SYMMETRIC POLYNEUROPATHY) in arms and legs.

Labs Arsenic levels elevated **in blood, urine, and hair.**

Imaging N/A

Gross Pathology N/A

Micro Pathology N/A

Treatment Penicillamine or orally administered 2,3-dimercaptosuccinic acid (DMSA).

Discussion Arsenic is used in a variety of settings, as pesticides, herbicides, rat poison, and in the metallurgic industry. The intoxication may be acute, with violent diarrhea, liver and renal necrosis, and shock potentially leading to death. In chronic exposure, the neurologic symptoms predominate over the gastrointestinal symptoms. The liver and kidney are also affected in chronic exposure.

ID/CC	A 6-year-old-girl is brought to the pediatric emergency room because she accidentally consumed large quantities of her sister's **"Vivarin"** stimulant pills.
HPI	The child, a healthy girl with no previous medical history, mistook the pills for candy which were in a non-child proof container nn the kitchen cabinets.
PE	VS: **tachycardia** (175); **hypotension** (BP 115/60). PE: **extreme restlessness, tremors,** and **nausea.**
Labs	CBC/Lytes/SMA7/UA are all normal.
Imaging	CXR/KUB are within normal limits for age.
Gross Pathology	N/A
Micro Pathology	N/A
Treatment	Monitor patient for ECG changes. Treat tachycardia and possible hypotension due to excess beta-1 and beta-2 stimulation with propranolol or esmolol.
Discussion	Caffeine is widely used as an appetite and **sleep suppressant** and as a **diuretic.** It has a wide therapeutic index; however, serious toxicity may result from accidental ingestion of large quantities. Beta blockers effectively reverse the cardiotoxic effects of excess catecholamine release and stimulation.

ID/CC   A 14-year old boy is brought to the ER by his anxious mother for **mild somnolence, mild stupor,** and **mild motor dysfunction.** The patient initially answers negatively to questions about drug use.

HPI   Upon further private questioning, he reveals that he had been "smoking a joint."

PE   VS: tachycardia; mild tachypnea. PE: **conjunctiva red and injected.**

Labs   UA: presence of **cannabinoids.**

Imaging   N/A

Gross Pathology   N/A

Micro Pathology   N/A

Treatment   There is no specific antidote for marijuana intoxication. Psychological disturbances can be treated with psychotherapy and adjunctive use of diazepam.

Discussion   The primary psychoactive agent in marijuana is delta-9-tetrahydrocannabinol, which is released during pyrolysis (smoking) of *Cannabis sativa.* Acute cannabis intoxication usually consists of a **subjective perception of relaxation** and **mild euphoria** accompanied by **mild impairment in thinking, concentration, and perceptual and psychosocial functions.** Chronic abusers may lose interest in common socially desirable goals. **Therapeutic effects include treatment for glaucoma, prevention of emesis** associated with cancer chemotherapy **and appetite stimulation (= "THE MUNCHIES").**

Carbon Monoxide Poisoning

ID/CC	A 29-year-old **mechanic** is brought to the emergency room after complaining of persistent **headache, nausea, and dizziness.**
HPI	He had been working all day, including overtime, indoors because of the cold weather, and felt **tired, dizzy,** and **nauseated.** He has otherwise been in good health.
PE	VS: tachycardia. PE: patient **lethargic** and **disoriented.**
Labs	**Carboxyhemoglobin** concentration of 38%. Pulse oximetry gives falsely normal readings.
Imaging	N/A
Gross Pathology	N/A
Micro Pathology	N/A
Treatment	Administer 100% oxygen until carboxyhemoglobin concentration is less than 5%. **Hyperbaric oxygen** therapy provides 100% O_2 under 2–3 atm, which may be useful in patients with severe intoxication.
Discussion	Carbon monoxide is an odorless, colorless, nonirritating gas that binds hemoglobin with an affinity 250 times greater than that of oxygen. For this reason, several minutes of exposure to a concentration of 1200 ppm may result in coma or death. Common sources include **automobile exhaust, fires,** and **kerosene stoves.** Survivors may suffer from permanent neurologic deficits ranging from memory loss to persistent vegetative states. Pulse oximetry gives falsely normal readings.

ID/CC   A 32-year-old stockbroker is brought to the ER after police find him **hiding in an alley.**

HPI   The patient had been at a **party** with several friends. He admits to indulging in cocaine from a new dealer for the past six hours.

PE   VS: hypertension (BP 180/95); **tachycardia** (160). PE: **restlessness; malnourishment; disorientation.**

Labs   N/A

Imaging   N/A

Gross Pathology   N/A

Micro Pathology   N/A

Treatment   Monitor vital signs and ECG for several hours. There are no specific antidotes for cocaine use. Propranolol may be used with a vasodilator for treatment of hypertension and tachyarrhythmias. Dialysis and hemoperfusion are not effective.

Discussion   Cocaine is a CNS stimulant and an inhibitor of neuronal catecholamine reuptake mechanisms; hence, its use results in a state of generalized sympathetic stimulation, with typical symptoms including **euphoria, anxiety, psychosis,** and **hyperactivity.** Severe **hypertension, ventricular tachycardia,** or **fibrillation** may also occur. **Angina pectoris** in a young, healthy person is suggestive of cocaine use. **Myocardial infarction** secondary to **coronary vasospasm** and thrombosis have been described as well.

ID/CC A 36-year-old male, an ear-nose and throat doctor, tells his psychiatrist that he has been feeling terribly **depressed** and **anxious** over the last three weeks.

HPI Patient has been in good health, but he recently entered into a **drug rehabilitation program** to **wean** himself **off cocaine.**

PE VS: tachycardic, normotensive, afebrile. PE: patient expresses concern over his increasing **lethargy, depression, hunger,** and **extreme cravings for stimulants** such as cocaine.

Labs Basic labwork and tox screen are all within normal limits. ECG: Sinus tachycardia

Imaging N/A

Gross Pathology N/A

Micro Pathology N/A

Treatment No definitive treatment exists to alleviate symptoms of cocaine withdrawal and associated cravings. Bromocriptine, a dopamine agonist that is used in Parkinson's disease, has been reported to diminish cocaine cravings.

Discussion Symptoms of cocaine withdrawal may be due to enhanced sensitivity of inhibitory receptors on dopaminergic neurons. Besides the physiologic withdrawal signs and symptoms, cocaine produces marked psychological dependency and withdrawal symptoms.

ID/CC	A 37-year-old male is brought to the ER by ambulance after collapsing while at work at a **metal-plating** factory.
HPI	The factory routinely uses **cyanide**-containing compounds in its chemical plating process. A co-worker reports that shortly before the patient collapsed, he complained of feeling **nauseous** and having a **headache**.
PE	VS: tachycardia (165); hypotension (BP 90/50). PE: patient experiencing **agonal respiration**, is unresponsive to external stimuli, and exudes a bitter **almond odor**.
Labs	Measured venous oxygen saturation elevated (due to markedly decreased oxygen uptake).
Imaging	N/A
Gross Pathology	N/A
Micro Pathology	N/A
Treatment	Treat all cyanide exposure as life-threatening. Give supplemental oxygen. Cyanide antidotes consist of amyl and sodium nitrates, which produce CN scavenging compounds. The scavengers (especially methemoglobin) accelerate the conversion of cyanide to thiocyanate.
Discussion	Cyanide is one of the most powerful poisons known, a chemical asphyxiant that binds to cytochrome oxidase, blocking the use of oxygen producing fulminant tissue hypoxia and death in seconds if inhaled or in minutes if ingested. It is used in the photographic, shoe polish, fumigation and metal plating industries. Free cyanide is metabolized to thiocyanate, which is less toxic and easily excreted in the urine. Exposure to cyanide gas can be rapidly fatal; however, toxicity due to ingestion of cyanide salts can be slowed with delayed absorption in the GI tract. Administer activated charcoal if accidental oral ingestion is suspected.

ID/CC A 40-year-old male who has been diagnosed with pemphigus vulgaris complains of **dysuria** and **increased urinary frequency.**

HPI The patient has no history of fever or gross hematuria. He is receiving monthly dexamethasone-**cyclophosphamide pulse therapy.**

PE VS: normal. PE: no pallor; lungs clear to auscultation; cardiac exam normal; abdomen soft, non tender; no suprapubic masses; no peritoneal signs; no tenderness in costovertebral angle.

Labs CBC: normocytic, normochromic **anemia;** mild leukopenia and thrombocytopenia. UA: **microscopic hematuria** but no bacteriuria.

Imaging N/A

Gross Pathology N/A

Micro Pathology N/A

Treatment Maintain good hydration and HCO_3 loading; epsilon amino caproic acid and MESNA may prevent hemorrhagic cystitis.

Discussion Cyclophosphamide is an alkylating agent that covalently cross-links DNA at guanine N-7 and requires bioactivation by the liver. It is used for lymphomas, breast and ovarian carcinmomas. Complications of cyclophosphamide use include **hemorrhagic cystitis, bladder fibrosis** and bladder carcinoma; **sterility; alopecia;** and inappropriate antidiuretic hormone (ADH) secretion. Cyclophosphamide needs to be converted to an active, toxic metabolite, **acrolein,** which is responsible for producing hemorrhagic cystitis.

ID/CC	A 45-year-old male who received a **renal transplant** four months ago comes for follow-up evaluation at the oncology unit complaining of headache and ringing in his ears. He was found to have **hypertension.**
HPI	He is currently taking multiple **immunosuppressive** drugs, including **cyclosporine.**
PE	VS: **hypertension** (150/110). PE: no jaundice; no pallor; cardiac exam normal; abdomen soft, non-tender; no abdominal masses; no peritoneal signs; fine hand **tremors** at rest noted.
Labs	Elevated cyclosporine levels; **elevated blood urea nitrogen (BUN) and serum creatinine.** Lytes: **hyperkalemia.** UA: **proteinuria.** ECG: peaked T waves (hyperkalemia).
Imaging	N/A
Gross Pathology	
Micro Pathology	Renal biopsy reveals presence of tubular lesions (vacuolization), atrophy, edema, microcalcifications, and absence of an acute cellular infiltrate that is characteristic of acute rejection.
Treatment	Reduction in cyclosporine dose with serial monitoring.
Discussion	Subacute cyclosporine nephrotoxicity is frequently seen in the first few weeks or months after renal transplantation, and it is often unclear whether the renal allograft dysfunction results from acute cellular rejection or cyclosporine toxicity. Renal biopsy is often necessary to guide therapy. Other clinical signs of acute cyclosporine toxicity include **hyperkalemia, hypertension, tremors, seizures, hirsutism, gingival hypertrophy,** and breast fibroadenomas.

ID/CC   A 54-year-old white female complains of intermittent **nausea and vomiting, headaches, fatigue,** and **blurred vision** over the past three months.

HPI   She describes objects as **appearing yellow** to her. She has a history of heart failure with **chronic digoxin** use, as well as **diuretics** (may induce hypokalemia).

PE   VS: **bradycardia** (48), normotensive, afebrile. PE: patient in no acute distress; slight increase in jugular venous pressure; S3; rales at lung bases; mild hepatomegaly; ankle edema.

Labs   CBC: normal. Lytes: **hypokalemia.** Elevated blood urea nitrogen (BUN); elevated creatinine. ECG: **Second degree A-V block with A-V junctional rhythm.**

Imaging   CXR shows moderate enlargement of the heart (due to long standing CHF), no signs of lung infection.

Gross Pathology   N/A

Micro Pathology   N/A

Treatment   Lower and space apart the dose. Correct hypokalemia.

Discussion   Digoxin is a cardiac glycoside that inhibits the Na-K ATP-ase of cell membranes, causing an increase in intracellular sodium, that causes an elevation in the intracellular calcium level thereby causing positive inotropy and chronotropy. **Renal failure may precipitate toxicity** at normal therapeutic doses (excretion is decreased). Hypokalemia is a frequent predisposing factor for toxicity. ECG changes may vary widely, A-V conduction disturbances, such as PAT with block are characteristic, as well as bigeminy, bradycardia, and flattened T waves.

ID/CC	A 42-year-old female presents to her family doctor because of increasing concern over a **facial rash** for the last two months that cannot be concealed with cosmetics.
HPI	She has also noticed **joint pains** in the knees and sacral region as well as diarrhea. For the past six months, she has been treated with **procainamide** for a supraventricular arrhythmia.
PE	Hyperpigmented, brownish **butterfly rash** over the malar region. Left lung is hypoventilated, with dullness to percussion and decreased fremitus (= PLEURAL EFFUSION); there is also a pericardial friction rub (due to pericarditis).
Labs	**Increased antinuclear antibody titer.** UA: **proteinuria** (> 0.5 mg/dL/day); presence of **cellular casts.** ECG: S-T, T wave changes (suggestive of pericarditis).
Imaging	CXR: small left pleural effusion and enlargement of cardiac silhouette (due to pericardial effusion).
Gross Pathology	N/A
Micro Pathology	N/A
Treatment	Discontinue procainamide therapy and consider other class IA antiarrhythmics. Lupus-like symptoms typically resolve.
Discussion	Approximately **one-third of patients** on **long-term procainamide** treatment develop a **lupus-like syndrome.** ANA titer is elevated in nearly all patients receiving this drug, which can also induce **pericarditis, pleuritis,** and pulmonary and renal disease. Other adverse effects include rash, **fever, diarrhea, hepatitis,** and **agranulocytosis.** SLE-like syndrome can also be produced by **hydralazine** and **isoniazid.**

ID/CC A 6-year-old boy is brought to the ER because of **severe vomiting.** The patient was "helping" his father in the garage when he saw an **antifreeze** bottle and, out of curiosity, he drank it.

HPI On arrival at the local pediatric emergency room, the boy started having tonic-clonic **seizures.**

PE VS: Patient is tachycardic (108/min), afebrile, with **hypotension** (BP 80/40). PE: He is **hyperventilating** and experiencing **convulsions.**

Labs CBC: Leukocytosis (13,000). **Ethylene glycol found in blood; metabolic acidosis with elevated** osmolar and **anion gap.** Hyponatremia, hyperkalemia. Blood urea nitrogen (BUN) and creatinine levels normal. ECG: **Premature ventricular beats.**

Imaging CXR: No evidence of bronchoaspiration of ethylene glycol.

Gross Pathology N/A

Micro Pathology N/A

Treatment **Administer ethanol** to saturate alcohol dehydrogenase, which prevents metabolism of ethylene glycol to its toxic metabolites. Administer **pyridoxine, folate, and thiamine,** (to attenuate the effects of toxic metabolites). Treat convulsions with diazepam and monitor vital signs. Hemodialysis can effectively remove ethylene glycol and correct acidosis and electrolyte abnormalities.

Discussion Ethylene glycol is the predominant component of antifreeze and may be used by alcoholics as an alcohol substitute. Because of its **sweet taste,** children and pets frequently ingest antifreeze. Its by-products may cause **metabolic acidosis, renal failure, and death.**

ID/CC A 34-year-old woman presents with her family practitioner complaining of **hearing loss, vertigo,** and inability to walk properly due to **lack of balance.**

HPI She is an otherwise healthy individual who underwent a left salpingectomy for pyosalpinx and was put on IV **gentamicin** for 10 days.

PE Well-hydrated, oriented, cooperative. Gait is ataxic and **Romberg test is positive.** Abdomen shows a well healed, infraumbilical midline scar, with no evidence of post-op hernia, infection or hematoma.

Labs **Elevated blood urea nitrogen (BUN)** and **serum creatinine;** fractional excretion of sodium markedly increased (> 1%). UA: **dark-brown granular casts** with free renal tubular epithelial cells and epithelial cell casts. ECG: normal sinus rhythm, no conduction abnormalities or signs of ischemia.

Imaging CXR: Fails to disclose any lung infection or cardiac abnormality to account for the patient's symptoms.

Gross Pathology N/A

Micro Pathology N/A

Treatment Supportive. Discontinuation of the aminoglycoside; resolution of acute episode may be delayed if patient remains hypovolemic, septic, or catabolic.

Discussion Gentamicin is an aminoglycoside, and thus shares the ototoxicity and nephrotoxicity of streptomycin, kanamycin, amikacin and tobramycin. Ototoxicity is mainly cochlear and marked by ataxia and vertigo. Nephrotoxicity is minimized if care is taken to hydrate the patient and keep serum levels therapeutic. Transient elevations of BUN and creatinine are common.

ID/CC   A 35-year-old plastic **surgeon** is rushed to the hospital by his wife after he is found lying comatose in his bed with a couple of **syringes lying on the floor** and his sleeve rolled up.

HPI   His wife states that her husband had been having serious financial problems; she has suspected drug use in light of recent **personality and mood changes**.

PE   On admission to ER, patient had a tonic-clonic **seizure; respiratory depression;** bradycardia; stupor; **pupils very constricted** (= PINPOINT PUPILS), cold skin; hypotension. Marked hyporeflexia; hypoactive bowel sounds; **needle "train track" marks** (stigmata of multiple previous injections).

Labs   ABG: hypoxemia; hypercapnia; respiratory acidosis. Urine tox screen positive for opioids.

Imaging   CXR: **noncardiogenic pulmonary edema** (edema without cardiomegaly).

Gross Pathology   Pulmonary congestion and edema; inflammatory neutrophilic infiltrate of arteries in brain and lung.

Micro Pathology   Brain cell swelling due to hypoxia.

Treatment   Establish a patent airway, assist ventilation, correct acid-base disorders, hypothermia, and hypotension. **Naloxone** as specific antagonist (naloxone may induce rapid opiate withdrawal), with follow-up in ICU.

Discussion   Heroin is a synthetic derivative of morphine that is abused as a recreational drug. Health professionals have a higher incidence of opiod abuse. Heroin abuse is a complex social disease that is linked with violence, prostitution, crime, antisocial behavior, and premature death; it may result in fatal overdose, endocarditis, fungal infections, abscess formation, anaphylaxis, and HIV transmission. Death may result from aspiration of gastric contents or from apnea.

ID/CC   A 2-year-old male is brought to the emergency room by his mother after a bout of **vomiting**.

HPI   The child has been seen by ER staff physicians in the past for **numerous episodes of vomiting and diarrhea.**

PE   VS: **tachycardia** (140); mild **hypotension** (BP 100/60). PE: **hyporeflexia; muscle weakness** and tenderness.

Labs   Lytes: serum **potassium low.** Blood urea nitrogen (BUN), creatine phosphokinase (CPK), and creatinine normal. ECG: no arrhythmias or conduction disturbances.

Imaging   N/A

Gross Pathology   N/A

Micro Pathology   N/A

Treatment   Treat fluid and electrolyte imbalances. Monitor ECG for changes and possible **arrhythmias** (cause of death).

Discussion   Ipecac syrup is an effective drug when induction of vomit is necessary due to ingestion of drugs and poisons, mainly in children. The safety margin is wide, but deaths have occurred when **fluid extract** of ipecac has been administered (much more concentrated than ipecac syrup). Chronic ipecac poisoning should be suspected in cases in which children are repeatedly brought in with symptoms such as these. Reports of such misuse in cases of "Munchausen's syndrome by proxy" have been recorded. Intoxication may result in cardiomyopathy and fatal arrhythmias (ipecac contains emetine).

ID/CC A 9-year-old male is brought to the emergency room after intentionally ingesting half a bottle of **iron tablets** (coated with plum-flavored sugar) six hours ago; he now complains of **abdominal pain**.

HPI He has been feeling weak and lightheaded, with palpitations and a metallic taste in his mouth. He had two episodes of **bluish-green vomit** followed by a large **hematemesis**.

PE VS: markedly **tachycardic** (120/min), **hypotensive** (90/50), afebrile. PE: Pulse is weak, patient is **pale and dehydrated**, with cold and clammy skin. Lungs are clear, abdomen is tender to deep palpation, predominantly in epigastrium, with no peritoneal signs. Neurologic exam normal. Rectal exam discloses black, tarry stool.

Labs Markedly elevated serum iron levels (> 500 mg/dL). Rose-wine colored urine. ABG: metabolic acidosis. BUN and creatinine elevated.

Imaging XR-Abdomen: shows multiple **radiopaque iron tablets** on GI tract from stomach to jejunum. Endoscopy: **diffuse hemorrhagic gastritis** with extensive necrosis and sloughing of mucosa.

Gross Pathology N/A

Micro Pathology N/A

Treatment Gastric lavage with bicarbonate solution (to form ferrous carbonate, which is not absorbed well) or induction of vomit. Treat acidosis, treat shock with IV fluids and **chelation** therapy with **deferoxamine.**

Discussion Mortality due to acute iron overdose may reach 25% or more, mainly in children. There may be marked dehydration and shock.

ID/CC A 22-year-old female presents to the ER with severe abdominal colics and a history of **profuse watery diarrhea** of several days' duration.

HPI She also complains of **dizziness** and a **desire to lose weight** (directed questioning discloses that she has been taking **magnesium sulfate** intermittently).

PE VS: **hypotension** (BP 80/45); temperature normal. PE: **skin shriveled; bowel sounds hyperactive.** Oliguric and lethargic.

Labs Lytes: hypokalemia, hyponatremia, hyperchloremia. ABG: normal anion gap metabolic acidosis.

Imaging N/A

Gross Pathology N/A

Micro Pathology N/A

Treatment Discontinue laxatives and offer counseling. Give IV glucose and electrolytes to restore fluid balance.

Discussion Laxative abuse remains a common way people attempt to lose weight, also abused commonly by psychiatric patients. Laxatives can interfere with the absorption of several medications such as tetracycline and calcium supplements. Laxatives may act by irritation of mucosa, direct neuronal stimulation, osmotic increase in the water content of stool, softening of stool by a detergent-like action, or by forming bulk. Continued abuse may lead to melanosis coli, colonic neuronal degeneration and the "lazy intestine syndrome". Patients with chronic constipation abuse laxatives to the point of being dependent on them for evacuation.

ID/CC	A 5-year-old male is brought to a medical clinic because of an episode of sudden, vigorous vomiting with no previous nausea (= PROJECTILE VOMITING) (due to encephalopathy); his mother adds that the child has been **behaving strangely** and has been **irritable.**
HPI	He also complains of **weakness in his hands and feet.** The boy lives in an **old house** that was recently renovated (old residential **paints and house dust** may contain toxic amounts of lead). He has had episodes of abdominal pain in the past.
PE	Pallor; lethargy; **foot drop** (due to peripheral neuropathy); retinal stippling; lines in gums (due to perivascular lead sulfide accumulation). **Wasting of muscles of hand with motor weakness** (hand grip 50%);
Labs	CBC: **hyperchromic, microcytic anemia with basophilic stippling.** Hyperuricemia. UA: **increased urinary coproporphyrin and aminolevulinic acid. Blood lead** and **free erythrocyte protoporphyrin levels elevated** glycosuria. **Hypophosphatemia.**
Imaging	XR-Long Bones: **broad bands** of **increased density** at metaphysis
Gross Pathology	Marked edema of brain; peripheral nerve segmental demyelinization.
Micro Pathology	Acid-fast intranuclear inclusion bodies in renal tubular cells, hepatocytes, and osteoclasts. BM Biopsy: **sideroblastic picture.**
Treatment	Separation from source of exposure; intramuscular chelation therapy with CaEDTA or DMSA orally, dimercaprol.
Discussion	Lead poisoning may be caused by gasoline; eating flaking wall paint (as occurs in pica); or using clay utensils with leaded glaze. Poisoning is more common in summer due to sun exposure with increased circulating porphyrins. Lead binds to disulfide groups, causing denaturation of enzymes, and inhibits ferrochelatase and delta-aminolevulinic acid dehydratase, thereby interfering with iron utilization in heme synthesis.

Malignant Hyperthermia

ID/CC	A 16-year-old female patient undergoes **surgery** to remove an inflamed appendix and has a rare anesthesia complication.
HPI	The father states that the patient's paternal uncle died of an anesthetic complication. The patient has had no prior surgery and received general anesthesia in the form of **halothane** and **succinylcholine.**
PE	VS: very high **fever** (39.8 °C); **hypertension** (BP 150/95). PE: generalized **muscular rigidity,** with difficulty breathing, anxiety and marked sweating.
Labs	CBC: Leukocytosis with neutrophilia Lytes: **hyperkalemia.** ABG: metabolic acidosis. Elevated CK.
Imaging	N/A
Gross Pathology	N/A
Micro Pathology	N/A
Treatment	Immediate treatment to lower body temperature, control acidosis, and restore electrolyte balance is critical to survival. IV dantrolene, (relaxes skeletal muscle by inhibiting release of calcium from sarcoplasmic reticulum). This allows muscle to relax and limits hyperthermia from muscle hyperactivity.
Discussion	Malignant hyperthermia is a highly lethal **genetically determined** myopathy (autosomal dominant trait). It is triggered by inhalation anesthetics (more comonly halothane), particularly those coupled with succinylcholine. The syndrome includes **tachycardia, hypertension, acidosis, hyperkalemia,** and **muscle rigidity**, and it apperars to be related to excess myoplasmic calcium.

ID/CC   A 28-year old male, professor of chemistry at the local high school, comes to the emergency room complaining of acute **retrosternal and epigastric pain** and frequent **vomiting** of blood-tinged material.

HPI   He admits to a **suicide attempt** through the ingestion of several teaspoons of **mercurium bichloride** (corrosive) from his chemistry lab. On arrival at the ER he had a **bloody, diarrheic** bowel movement.

PE   VS: **Hypotension**, tachycardia. PE: Pallor, skin is cold and clammy, tongue is whitish, patient is confused, **oliguric and dyspneic**, Moderate abdominal tenderness; **grayish discoloration of buccal mucosa.**

Labs   **Elevated serum creatinine and blood urea nitrogen (BUN).** UA: presence of tubular casts. Fractional excretion of sodium markedly increased; serum hemoglobin levels markedly elevated.

Imaging   N/A

Gross Pathology   Acute tubular necrosis, acute irritative colitis with mucosal necrosis with sloughing and hemorrhage.

Micro Pathology   N/A

Treatment   Specific chelation therapy with dimercaprol and succimer (dimercapto-succinic acid); supportive management of acute tubular necrosis.

Discussion   Mercury, in its multiple forms, is toxic to human beings. Organic mercury is the most toxic. Acute toxicity is exemplified with this case. Chronic mercury exposure produces proteinuria, stomatitis, and CNS signs, mostly in children. These signs include insomnia, irritability, ataxia, nystagmus and convulsions.

ID/CC   A 46-year-old **homeless alcoholic** is brought to the ER by two of his friends in a **confused, incoherent state;** he has been in the ER on many previous occasions.

HPI   He appears unkempt and, as usual, **smells heavily of alcohol.** He is very anxious, constantly repeating that he **cannot see clearly.**

PE   VS: tachycardia; normotension. PE: patient confused as to time, person, and place; speech incoherent; **rapid respirations** (to try to compensate severe acidosis by lowering PO_2); no meningeal or peritoneal signs; no focal neurologic deficit; **marked photophobia** when eye reflex is elicited; papilledema.

Labs   CBC/Lytes: normal. Amylase normal (methanol may produce an acute pancreatitis); liver function tests slightly altered (due to chronic alcoholic liver disease). LP: CSF normal. ABGs: **pH 7.2** (= ACIDOSIS). **Anion gap increased; serum osmolarity elevated** (due to osmotically active methanol). ECG: normal.

Imaging   CXR: normal. CT - Brain: normal.

Gross Pathology   N/A

Micro Pathology   Retinal edema with degeneration of ganglion cells; optic nerve atrophy after acute event has subsided.

Treatment   IV ethanol (ethanol competes with methanol for alcoholic dehydrogenase, having a much greater affinity for the enzyme). Dialysis, folinic acid.

Discussion   Methyl alcohol (= METHANOL) is degraded by dehydrogenase to formaldehyde and formic acid, both of which are toxic compounds that cause a high-anion-gap metabolic acidosis together with ocular lesions that may lead to blindness (due to retinal and optic nerve atrophy).

ID/CC   A 46-year-old girl scout guide presents to the emergency room of the local rural hospital with excessive **thirst**, weakness, protracted **vomiting, acute abdominal pain** and **severe diarrhea.**

HPI   She has been in good health and states that during the camping trip she ate some **wild mushrooms** (about six hours ago) that she had hand picked.

PE   VS: **tachycardia** (165); **hypotension** (BP 85/40). PE: lethargy; disorientation, skin is cold and cyanotic, hyperactive bowel sounds on abdominal exam.

Labs   **Liver transaminases and bilirubin elevated; prothrombin time (PT) increased. Increased BUN and creatinine.**

Imaging   N/A

Gross Pathology   N/A

Micro Pathology   N/A

Treatment   Thioctic acid, hemodyalisis, treat fluid and electrolyte losses aggressively. There are no proven antidotes for amatoxin poisoning. Liver may be so damaged so as to have to consider transplant.

Discussion   There are many species of toxic mushrooms with clinical pictures according to the specific poison involved. The most commonly involved in the US are *Amanita phalloides* (delayed intoxication) and *Amanita muscaria* (rapid toxicity). According to mushroom type, toxins may produce antocholinergic effects (mydriasis, tachycardia, blurred vision) or muscarinic effects (salivation, myosis, bradycardia). These types of mushrooms are often picked and eaten by **amateur foragers.** Toxins are highly stable and remain after cooking. They are absorbed by intestinal cells, and subsequent cell death and sloughing occurs within 8–12 hours of ingestion. Severe hepatic and renal necrosis is also a common effect of these toxins.

ID/CC	A 48-year-old male complains to his doctor about increasing anxiety, **insomnia, irritability** and **severe cravings** for cigarettes.
HPI	The patient, a 2-pack a day smoker for 20 years, recently **quit smoking.** He claims that he is **no longer able to relax,** and has been having problems with his wife and at work due to impulsiveness.
PE	VS: **tachycardia** (155); **hypertension** (BP 165/110). PE: patient **anxious** and **sweating.** Rest of examination is within normal limits.
Labs	CBC: Increased hematocrit. Hypertrygliceridemia, hypercholesterolemia.
Imaging	CXR: Signs of chronic bronchitis and emphysema.
Gross Pathology	N/A
Micro Pathology	N/A
Treatment	Gradually reducing the dose of nicotine either in **transdermal patches** or with **nicotine-containing gum** is helpful in weaning smokers from nicotine addiction. Group therapy, hypnosis, psychological consultation.
Discussion	Nicotine produces **serious addiction** and long-lasting cravings upon quitting. Nicotine produces euphoriant effects; however, tolerance develops rapidly. The psychological dependence of nicotine is very severe, and a major impediment to quitting the tobacco habit. It is sometimes stronger than the physiologic dependence.

ID/CC   A 22-year old white female professional skier goes to the emergency room complaining of severe **malaise, dizziness,** jaundice, **very low urinary volumes,** and **fatigue.**

HPI   Following a recent skiing accident, in which she sprained her shoulder and knee, she took a total of 20 tablets of **diclofenac** over a three day-period.

PE   VS: mild hypotension (100/60), afebrile. PE: severe dehydration. There is tenderness to palpation in epigastric area, pitting **ankle and palpebral edema.**

Labs   Lytes: **hyperkalemia.** Markedly **elevated blood urea nitrogen** (BUN); and **serum creatinine;** urine osmolality increased; fractional excretion of sodium less than 1%. UA: proteinuria.

Imaging   US-Abdomen: normal-sized, normal-appearing kidneys.

Gross Pathology   N/A

Micro Pathology   N/A

Treatment   Volume replacement, metabolic correction, immediate withdrawal of NSAIDs, avoidance of all nephrotoxic medications.

Discussion   NSAID use, such as diclofenac, can lead to acute renal failure via two mechanisms: (1) unopposed renal vasoconstriction by angiotensin II and norepinephrine; and (2) reduction in cardiac output caused by the associated rise in systemic vascular resistance (an effect that is opposite to the beneficial decrease in cardiac afterload induced by vasodilators). Thus, inhibition of prostaglandin synthesis by an NSAID can lead to **reversible renal ischemia, a decline in glomerular hydrostatic pressure** (the major driving force for glomerular filtration), and **acute renal failure.**

ID/CC   A 32-year-old male, lead drummer of a popular rock band, presents to the emergency room with **high fever, running nose** and **severe diarrhea** as well as abdominal pain.

HPI   He is a chronic user of multiple drugs and had been a **heroin addict** for two years until last week when he decided to quit.

PE   VS: **tachycardia** (165); **hypertension** (BP 160/90). Patient has **lacrimation and rhinorrhea**, is thin, **anxious,** malnourished, and **sweating** profusely. He exhibits generalized **piloerection** ("GOOSE-BUMPS"). Abdomen shows tenderness to deep palpation, but there is no muscle rigidity or peritoneal signs.

Labs   CBC/Lytes: normal.

Imaging   CXR/KUB: Within normal limits.

Gross Pathology   N/A

Micro Pathology   N/A

Treatment   Treat electrolyte abnormalities resulting from severe diarrhea. Monitor vital signs. Consider methadone substitution; clonidine.

Discussion   Tolerance to opioids is a true cellular adaptive response on many levels, including Ca^{2+} flux, G protein synthesis, and adenyl cyclase inhibition. Withdrawal effects consist of **rhinorrhea, yawning, piloerection, lacrimation, diarrhea, vomiting, anxiety,** and **hostility.** These effects begin within 6 hours of the last dose and may last 4–5 days. Cravings for opiates may last for many years.

ID/CC A 30-year-old **farmer** is brought to the emergency room with **severe abdominal cramps** and **vomiting.**

HPI The patient is also **restless** and is **salivating profusely.** He has been working with a new pesticide for the past 3 months.

PE Patient is nearly **stuporous; cyanosis** with marked respiratory distress; **miosis present bilaterally; marked salivation** and **lacrimation;** moderate dehydration; **hyperactive bowel sounds; incontinence** with regard to both **urine and feces.**

Labs ABGs: marked **hypoxemia** with **hypercapnia;** uncompensated **respiratory acidosis. Prerenal azotemia** on renal function tests. Lytes: **hyperkalemia.**

Imaging CXR is normal.

Gross Pathology N/A

Micro Pathology N/A

Treatment Specific therapy includes administration of **atropine** (to offset cholinergic effects) and **pralidoxime** (chemically restores acetylcholinesterase if administered early); supportive management for respiratory support and hemodialysis.

Discussion Organophosphates like parathion and carbamates are widely used as pesticides, and several nerve agents developed for chemical warfare are rapid-acting and potent organophosphates. All of these toxins **inhibit the enzyme acetylcholinesterase,** preventing the breakdown of acetylcholine at cholinergic synapses. Whereas the **organophosphates may cause permanent damage** to the enzyme, **carbamates have a transient and reversible effect.**

ID/CC   A 22-year-old male is brought to the emergency room by the police after he began **threatening people** at a nightclub.

HPI   Friends reported that the patient had taken **phencyclidine** ("angel dust") earlier that evening.

PE   PE: gait is **ataxic**, eyes show nystagmus. Patient behaves **acutely psychotic** and **paranoid**; (claims that "small, green men" are monitoring his movements).He repeats every thing that the doctor tells him (ECHOLALIA), any small noise bothers him out of proportion to intensity (HYPERACUSIS).

Labs   CBC/Lytes: normal.

Imaging   N/A

Gross Pathology   N/A

Micro Pathology   N/A

Treatment   Sedation with diazepam or **haloperidol and a quiet environment** is helpful to reduce severe agitation. Monitor temperature and vital signs to guard against hyperthermia and consequent rhabdomyolysis.

Discussion   Phencyclidine (PCP) blocks NMDA glutamate receptors and can induce a psychosis similar to schizophrenia. PCP is a **dissociative anesthetic** with properties similar to ketamine. It produces a generalized loss of pain perception and also has CNS-stimulant effects. **Hypertension, tachycardia, hyperthermia, rigidity, convulsions,** and **coma** may result from severe intoxication. Violent behavior is characteristic.

ID/CC A 58-year-old male is brought to the emergency room with **acute hypotension, bradycardia,** and **difficulty breathing.**

HPI He has been receiving **propranolol** for hypertension and recently increased his dose on medical prescription.

PE VS: **hypotension** (BP 90/50); **bradycardia** (55). PE: Patient is lethargic, with slowness of movements, lung field auscultation reveals mild wheezing.

Labs Lytes: hyperkalemia. Hypoglycemia. ECG: normal QRS duration with **increased PR interval** (A-V BLOCK).

Imaging CXR: no evidence of lung infiltrates, effusion or masses. Cardiac silhouette is normal.

Gross Pathology N/A

Micro Pathology N/A

Treatment Monitor vital signs, treat bradycardia with atropine and isoproterenol as needed. Treat bronchospasm with bronchodilator. Glucagon should also be administered.

Discussion Beta-blocker toxicity varies widely in clinical presentation. Severe reactions to beta blockers are known to occur at normal therapeutic dosages. **Cardiac disturbances are common,** such as bradycardia and A-V block, but CNS toxicity, including respiratory arrest and coma, may also occur. Beta blockers may exacerbate or precipitate an attack of asthma; impotence is another side effect. Other drugs may present with similar toxic reactions, including antihypertensive agents, digitalis, tricyclic antidepressants, and calcium channel blockers.

ID/CC   A 6-year-old boy is brought by his parents to the emergency room in a **comatose state.**

HPI   The child had been suffering from **chickenpox** and had been given **aspirin** by the family physician for fever.

PE   VS: **fever.** PE: comatose child with **papulovesicular rash** all over body; fundus shows **marked papilledema;** no icterus, moderate hepatomegaly, asterixis.

Labs   **Marked hypoglycemia. Increased blood ammonia concentration; elevated aspartate transaminase (AST) and alanine transaminase (ALT); prolonged prothrombin time (PT);** serum bilirubin normal. LP (done after lowering raised intracranial pressure): normal CSF.

Imaging   CT: findings suggestive of **generalized cerebral edema.**

Gross Pathology   Severe cerebral edema, acute hepatic necrosis.

Micro Pathology   Liver biopsy reveals microvesicular steatosis with little or no inflammation; electron microscopy shows marked mitochondrial abnormalities.

Treatment   Specific therapy not available. Supportive measures include lactulose to control hyperammonemia, fresh frozen plasma to replenish clotting factors, mannitol or dexamethasone to lower increased intracranial pressure, and mechanical ventilation. Exchange transfusion; dialysis.

Discussion   Although the cause of the highly lethal Reye's syndrome (hepatoencephalopathy) is unknown, epidemiologic evidence strongly links this disorder with outbreaks of viral disease, especially influenza B and chickenpox. Epidemiologic evidence has also prompted the Surgeon General and the American Academy of Pediatrics Committee on Infectious Diseases to recommend that **salicylates not be given to children with chickenpox or influenza B.**

ID/CC   A 5-year-old female is brought by her parents to the pediatric ER with **severe nausea, hematemesis,** and **abdominal pain.**

HPI   She had been playing "candy maker" in her parents' room, and an **open aspirin bottle** was found on the floor. The child is otherwise healthy.

PE   VS: **Marked increase in respiratory frequency** (HYPERVENTILATION), **febrile,** normotensive. PE: Flushed face, lethargy; **disorientation; dehydration, generalized petechia,** abdominal pain.

Labs   CBC: **Thrombocytopenia. Elevated prothrombin time (PT).** Lytes: normal. ABG: Respiratory alkalosis.

Imaging   CXR: Within normal limits for age.

Gross Pathology   N/A

Micro Pathology   N/A

Treatment   Antacids may be used for gastrointestinal upset. Fluid losses should be replaced. Administer activated charcoal. Based on specific acid-base disorder, treat accordingly.

Discussion   Aspirin toxicity may be pronounced in doses that are only five times the therapeutic amount. Decreased prostaglandin production results in decreased pain, inflammation, and fever. Acute ingestion may affect the integrity of the gastric mucosa and alter blood flow, which are prostaglandin-dependent processes. Diagnosis often depends on patient history, since quantitative levels are often not available. Salicylates stimulate the breathing center, thereby producing hyperventilation and respiratory alkalosis. Salicylates produce a metabolic acidosis, as well as ketosis, so at different times during an intoxication and depending on the dosage, there will be different, often mixed, acid-base disorders.

Thalidomide Exposure

ID/CC A newborn infant has **underdeveloped limbs** consisting of **short stumps without fingers or toes** (= PHOCOMELIA).

HPI Her mother took a drug for anxiety and insomnia during the first trimester of pregnancy; the drug was **thalidomide.**

PE As described.

Labs N/A

Imaging N/A

Gross Pathology N/A

Micro Pathology N/A

Treatment N/A

Discussion Thalidomide is a well-known teratogen that was widely used during the first trimester of pregnancy as an agent for insomnia because of its quick sleep-inducing effect. It caused phocomelia, in which a child's limbs resemble the **flippers of a seal,** with failure of development of the long bones of the extremities. Several thousand children were born with this abnormality, making the medical community painfully aware of first trimester teratogens. Thalidomide induces abortions and multiple other fetal abnormalities.

ID/CC
A 48-year-old patient being treated for a large abscess in his lower back develops **oliguria, hematuria,** and an extensive **erythematous skin rash.**

HPI
The patient has been treated according to culture and sensitivity of the pus from the abscess against *Staphylococcus aureus* with **methicillin.** He has no history of allergy to any medications.

PE
VS: fever(38.2°C), mild tachycardia. PE: erythematous **skin rash;** rales auscultated over left lung base.

Labs
Increased Serum creatinine and **blood urea nitrogen** (BUN). CBC: eosinophilia. Blood culture sterile. UA: mild **proteinuria;** sterile pyuria; urinary sediment shows abundant eosinophils and no bacteria.

Imaging
US-Abdomen: normal kidneys.

Gross Pathology
N/A

Micro Pathology
Renal biopsy shows evidence of **tubulointerstitial disease;** inflammatory infiltrate in interstitium consists of a large number of eosinophils in addition to neutrophils, lymphocytes, and plasma cells.

Treatment
Alternative antibiotic therapy and supportive management; cessation of offending drug often reverses disease.

Discussion
Drugs commonly associated with acute tubulointerstitial disease include **penicillin, ampicillin, thiazides, rifampin, methicillin,** and **cimetidine.** This type II hypersensitivity reaction is often reversed with cessation of offending drug; if it is not reversed, it may progress to renal failure.

ID/CC   A 59-year-old female visits her family doctor complaining of **chronic fatigue, muscle weakness** and **cramps.**

HPI   She has been receiving **furosemide** for the treatment of essential hypertension for more than one year now.

PE   VS: **tachycardia.** PE: **dehydration,** somnolence, muscle weakness, deep tendon reflexes are slow.

Labs   Elevated uric acid. Lytes: **decreased potassium and magnesium.** ECG: Flattened T waves and prominent U waves (due to hypokalemia)

Imaging   N/A

Gross Pathology   N/A

Micro Pathology   N/A

Treatment   Treatment consists of replacement of fluid and electrolyte losses. Monitor ECG for cardiac abnormalities.

Discussion   Significant dehydration and electrolyte imbalance may occur in loop diuretic overdose. These compounds (**furosemide, bumetanide,** and **ethacrynic acid**) are potent diuretics that inhibit the Na/K/2Cl transport system, which can result in **hypokalemic metabolic alkalosis.** K replacement and correction of hypovolemia can reverse this toxicity. Additional adverse effects include **ototoxicity, hyperuricemia, allergic reactions,** and **hypomagnesemia.**

ID/CC
A 40-year-old woman who suffers from **chronic arthritis and headache** for which she takes several types of pain killers containing **phenacetin**, says she had an episode of severe, colicky pain in the right lumbar region in the morning.

HPI
She adds that the pain radiated to the groin, her **urine was bloody,** and she **passed a small piece of soft tissue**, after which the pain subsided. The patient has not consumed any fluids since this episode. She also has a history of **recurrent urinary tract infections (UTIs).**

PE
VS: no fever; hypertension. PE: **anemia;** costovertebral angle reveals no tenderness; neither kidney palpable.

Labs
CBC: normocytic, normochromic anemia. **Serum creatinine and blood urea nitrogen (BUN) elevated.** UA: **gross hematuria;** sediment with no crystals. Tissue that patient passed measures about 4 mm and is **gray and necrotic;** no crystalline material demonstrated.

Imaging
IVP: classic "ring sign" of papillary necrosis— **radiolucent, sloughed papilla surrounded by radiodense contrast material in calyx.** US-Abdomen: bilateral small kidneys. CT: presence of papillary necrosis.

Gross Pathology
N/A

Micro Pathology
Papillary necrosis and tubulointerstitial inflammation on renal biopsy.

Treatment
Total **cessation of analgesic use,** adequate hydration, and control of hypertension. Regular surveillance of urine cytology will detect uroepithelial tumors, which may arise after discontinuation of analgesic agent.

Discussion
Seen in middle aged females with migraines or rheumatic diseases, who take large amounts of analgesics. Usually there is a psychologic component in the compulsion to take them.

About the Authors

VIKAS BHUSHAN, MD

Vikas is a diagnostic radiologist in Los Angeles and the series editor for *Underground Clinical Vignettes*. His interests include traveling, reading, writing, and world music. He is single and can be reached at vbhushan@aol.com.

CHIRAG AMIN, MD

Chirag is an orthopedics resident at Orlando Regional Medical Center. He can be reached at chiragamin@aol.com.

TAO LE, MD

Tao is completing a medicine residency at Yale-New Haven Hospital and is applying for a fellowship in allergy and immunology. He is married to Thao, who is a pediatrics resident. He can be reached at taotle@aol.com.

HOANG NGUYEN

Hoang (Henry) is a third-year MD/PhD student at Northwestern University. Henry is single and lives in Chicago, where he spends his free time writing, reading, and enjoying music. He can be reached at hbnguyen@nwu.edu.

JOSE M. FIERRO, MD

Jose (Pepe) is beginning a med/peds residency at Brookdale University Hospital in New York. He is a general surgeon from Mexico who worked extensively in Central Africa. His interests include world citizenship and ethnic music. He is married and can be reached at fierro@mail.dsinet.com.mx.

KRIS ALDEN

Kris is a fourth-year MD/PhD student at University of Illinois - Chicago. Kris is single and lives in Chicago, where he enjoys reading science journals and sampling Chicago's eateries. He can be reached at kalden@uic.edu.

VISHAL PALL, MBBS

Vishal recently completed medical school and internship in Chandigarh, India. He hopes to begin his residency training in the US in July 1999. He can be reached at mona@puniv.chd.nic.in.